Richard Adams

NATURE THROUGH THE SEASONS

Illustrated by David A. Goddard

Science texts by Max Hooper
Illustrated by Adrian Williams

KESTREL BOOKS

In the science texts and captions all measurements have been shown according to the metric system and all temperatures are given in Centigrade. A conversion table appears after the index on page 108.

Kestrel Books
An imprint of Penguin Books Ltd, Harmondsworth, Middlesex, England

Copyright © 1975 by The Felix Gluck Press Limited, Twickenham England

Text Copyright © 1975 for pages 8-9, 10-11, 18-19, 26-27, 34-35, 42-43, 50-51, 58-59, 66-67, 74-75, 82-83, 90-91, 98-99 by Richard Adams.

First published 1975
ISBN 0 7226 5007 8

This edition is not to be sold in the USA

Colouring Research and Assistance by Katharine Riley
Leaf-print on Endpapers by Stephen Lee

Designed and produced by The Felix Gluck Press

Photosetting by Apex Photosetting, London
Printed in Holland by 4P Drukkerij Reclame B.V. Rotterdam

CONTENTS

Introduction

Very old are the woods;
And the buds that break
Out of the brier's boughs
When March winds wake,
So old with their beauty are—
Oh, no man knows
Through what wild centuries
Roves back the rose.

It is this timeless sense of a joy which is almost fear that many people—or so it has often appeared to me—find they cannot feel, even when alone in a wood or by a stream. Perhaps they are still thinking too much of their own affairs. Or they may be trying too hard—having decided that they want to discover some particular thing which a book has told them is rare. They may have made or been given a list of things to look out for, and they hope to be able to tick them all off, if they can. This is the wrong approach—or so I believe. Nature is not a competition. It doesn't really matter, when you go out, if you don't identify anything. What matters is the feeling heart, and the only point of identifying things is to help you (if it does) to derive more joy and pleasure from them. One can take as much pleasure in the commonest as in the rarest things. A robin is as beautiful as a lesser spotted woodpecker, and a primrose as a bee orchid. Interesting details often go unnoticed even in familiar things; for example, in the primroses, of which there are two kinds, the thrum-eyed and the pin-eyed. The thrum-eyed bloom has a minute cluster of yellow stamens in the centre; the pistil in the pin-eyed bloom is like a tiny, round, green table. Is this sort of thing worth noticing? If it gives you pleasure to notice it, yes.

Not to be impatient, not to be in a hurry, not to be disappointed—in the weather, say; or in a bird that is not to be seen, though it was yesterday—this sort of resilient temperament is not always easy to develop. Yet Nature herself is infinitely patient, resilient and undiscriminating.

Some people prefer, when they are in the country, to engage in some activity—such as fishing, climbing or photography—as well as looking at nature. Then, if nothing much turns up (which is often the way), one has still had a good day out. If it suits you, this is certainly a good plan. Fishing, riding, walking—anything that is quiet and relaxed, and does not interfere with looking and listening.

Of course there are different kinds of patience. The nature lover's should be the wary, alert sort, for somehow it always seems to be at unexpected moments that the memorable things happen—a dog stoat comes trotting out of the long grass, a green woodpecker flies directly overhead, or a copse through which we take a short cut turns out to contain an autumn crocus. But even when unusual things don't happen, the harebell and milkwort (and even the ragwort) remain beautiful flowers, and a magpie, flickering black-and-white across a lane and cocking its long tail as it alights, is well worth admiring. John Clare, the son of a country labourer, who became perhaps the greatest—certainly the most lovable—English nature poet (and remained a poor and an unlucky man all his life), used to lie in the long grass and watch the summer insects—apparently for hours at a time. To read his nature poems is to find a kind of human expression of that unquestioning acceptance of life which is shown by the birds and animals themselves. The golden-crested wren does not know that he is beautiful, or that we admire him; and the thrush's song is the only one he knows. There is something intensely moving in seeing the blackcap, who twice a year undertakes a long, dangerous, migratory flight and whose expectation of life is about three or four years if he is lucky, sitting on a green branch, singing as though the world were one eternal May morning. In fact, I don't know anything better.

Richard Adams

Each of David Goddard's landscape illustrations in this book is preceded by a text by Richard Adams and followed by scientific explanations by Max Hooper.

The Wood in Spring

Some of the things which give me most pleasure in early spring—that's to say, from March or sometimes even earlier—are very common. This is part of their charm—to know that thousands of people, for hundreds of years past, have noticed and delighted in them. I love the very black, almost unnatural smoothness of the ash buds; or a thrush singing at nightfall against a chilly, green sky. My particular favourite is the great tit—one of the first signs of early spring, as early as the snowdrop. He likes a high song-post—perhaps the top of a silver birch—and here he 'rings his bell', as they say ('*hi*-tatty, *hi*-tatty, *hi*-tatty). Monotonous it would be, if one were not so glad to hear it. The blue tit, on the other hand, seldom bothers about a song-post. If ever he does, it will be a much lower one—a bramble sticking out of the hedge, perhaps. But usually he just sings as he goes about his business in the wind—two notes and a quiet trill, which I always think of as 'Heigh, ho, go-and-get-another-bit-of-moss'.

Any time on a fine day in late March you can hope to hear the chiff-chaff. He's not a tit; he's a migrant warbler who comes north to this country from abroad, and when you hear him you can be sure summer's on the way. He likes a high post too, and he just goes 'chiff, chaff, chiff, chaff' (and sometimes 'chiff, chiff': I suppose he likes a change, such as it is). He always ends with the 'chiff'.

As for flowers, who isn't happy to see the snowdrops (how many petals has a snowdrop—and how many colours are there in the bloom?); the celandines, which look as if they had just been varnished; the frail, pale wood anemones (which die almost immediately if picked); and the coltsfoot, the first 'dandelion' of the spring, with its spurred stalk?

When I was a little boy (before Hitler's war) we often made expeditions to bring back flowers of one kind and another, and very often from woods. There was always a spring expedition for bluebells—I remember being taught that they are marked 'I, I' (Alas! Alas!) in memory of the death of Hyakinthos of ancient Greece—though I never could find that they were: perhaps Greek bluebells are different—and bluebells I still love, both for their colour and for their beautiful, cool, faint scent. There were primroses, too, and together with these we always used to pick a few plants of dog's mercury; the shiny green to show off the pale yellow. One afternoon, when I was picking primroses near the bank of a stream, a rabbit came running through the field on the opposite bank, plunged in and swam across: and yet people will tell you that rabbits don't swim. You never know what you may see, but the golden rule, of course, is to keep quiet—if you can.

This is probably as good a moment as any to say that if you mean business—or just pleasure, for that matter—it is important to get hold of a good book on wild flowers. There are many simplified and incomplete books, but my own view is that while one is about it, one might as well go the whole hog and get a definitive work that is going to last all one's life; for then one doesn't have to cut and come again, and can be certain that every flower one finds will definitely be in the book. The best is the Rev. Keble Martin's, which is beautifully illustrated in accurate colour and a real pleasure to possess; but those good old veterans, Bentham and Hooker, have a lot to recommend them too. It's not essential to take a course in botany—plenty of it rubs off on you as you go on looking and learning.

Key to Illustration on pages 12-13

ANIMALS

1 Roe deer and fawn 2 Badgers 3 Rabbit 4 Squirrel 5 Green woodpecker 6 Great tit
7 Jay 8 Magpie 9 Tawny owl 10 Blue tit 11 Pearl-bordered fritillary 12 Brimstone (male)
13 Common blue 14 Small copper 15 Wood white 16 Ladybird

PLANTS AND TREES

17 Wych elm 18 Ash 19 Oak 20 Maple 21 Beech 22 Sessile oak 23 Rowan
24 Silver birch 25 Elm 26 Sycamore 27 Small-leaved lime 28 Tree stump of oak
29 Tree stump of elm 30 Holly 31 Hawthorn 32 Hazel 33 Bluebell 34 Wood sorrel
35 Primrose 36 Wood anemone 37 Lesser periwinkle 38 Dog's mercury 39 Ivy 40 Bracken

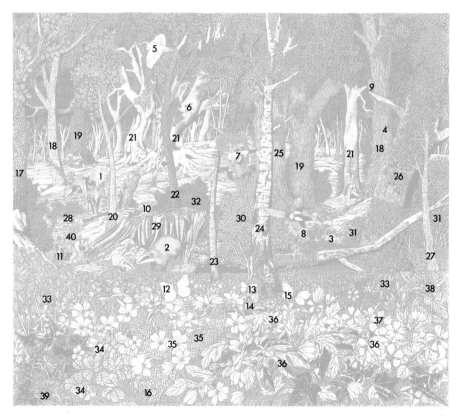

11

The Light Switch

As winter turns into spring, the length of the day changes, and this is very important to animals and particularly to plants. When you go to bed on a winter evening it is dark outside and when you wake up in the morning, unless you get up very late, it is still rather dark. But as winter ends and the spring flowers begin to appear in large numbers—usually in March— you will find that it is much lighter in the evening and completely light when you get up. March is the month when spring really begins. Catkins appear on pussy willow and hazelnut, and moths begin their search for nectar, the sweet honey-like liquid in the catkins. Birds begin to nest. By the time that April arrives, trees are beginning to come into leaf, bluebells cover the ground in the wood clearings and primroses begin to flower. Migrant birds that have spent the winter in warmer countries begin to return and the cuckoo can be heard for the first time.

But why do these birds and plants behave in this way—what switches them on in the spring? For many of them it is the change in the length of daylight. The new flowers, the feeding moths and the returning birds all respond to the photoperiodic (light-time) switch. At the beginning of March we have about eleven hours of daylight, but by the end of May we have about sixteen hours. We can make experiments to find out how the longer day affects living things and we shall find that they behave in very different ways.

If you go to a near-by wood in late spring, you will almost certainly find a grass called wood meadow-grass. It is not very big and not particularly exciting, with its spike of grass flowers rather flattened from side to side. But a lot of experiments have been made to see how it behaves. If you grew this grass in a box with an electric light and switched the light on for

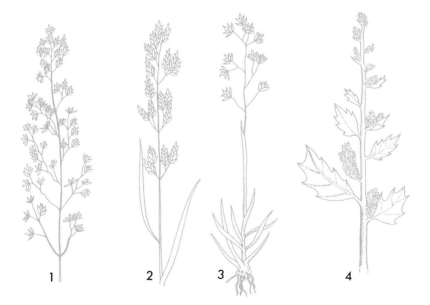

1 2 3 4

Meadow-grasses are members of a group of grasses all rather similar, with about two hundred species in the world. The smooth meadow-grass (1), and its relations, flat-stalked meadow-grass (2), and woodland meadow-grass (3), is a 'long-day plant'. The red goosefoot, also shown here (4), is not a grass, and is a 'short-day plant'.

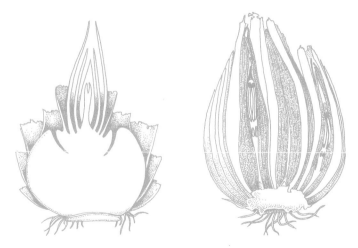

The crocus corm (left) and the daffodil bulb look rather alike in shape, but the corm is a swollen underground stem, while the bulb is formed of swollen leaves.

only ten hours every day you would find that the grass did not flower. But if you kept the light on for fifteen hours every day the wood meadow-grass would produce flowers just as it does in the wood. So we can say that somewhere between ten and fifteen hours there is a special amount of light each day which makes the grass flower. Nobody knows exactly what this length of time (called *the critical length*) is, and it may vary between slightly different types (*races*) of the same grass.

Not all plants are switched on to flowering by long periods of light. Some need very short days. There is a plant called red goosefoot, growing in farmyards and waste places, which is one of these. If you switched on the light for only eight hours it would flower within three weeks while it was only a little seedling; but if you left on the light for twenty hours every day the red goosefoot would grow very tall, perhaps two metres, and still not flower.

Botanists, who want to be more precise, would call the wood meadow-grass a long-day plant and red goosefoot a short-day plant. But just to make things more difficult, there are some plants which actually get switched on *because of* the change from long to short days or from short to long days—and with these plants it would be no use growing them in a long period of light (like the wood meadow-grass) or in a short period of light (like the red goosefoot). In neither case would they flower. Wheat (which is used to make bread) and rye, which is used to make another type of darker bread, are like this, and it is the change in the length of day from short to long in spring that acts as a switch and makes them flower.

With many of the plants that flower in the woods in the spring— primroses, bluebells, lilies of the valley—it is the change in the length of the daylight that switches them on, and then the cold winter days hold them back so that the flowers do not appear until the following spring when the weather is warmer. The wood anemone, for example, has very tiny flowers inside it as early as August or September but the flowers do not appear until April. The tulips and daffodils in the garden are much the same as the wood anemone—they also have tiny flowers inside them in the autumn and winter. If you cut open a tulip or daffodil bulb in September or October you can see the young flowers, or if you grow the bulbs inside a warm cupboard you can force the flowers to grow by Christmas.

15

Butterflies and Moths

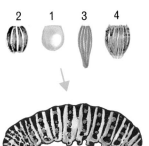

Butterflies and moths pass through four stages in their lives. Eggs are laid and these develop into caterpillars. Soon the caterpillar becomes 'sleepy' and may burrow or attach itself by a thread to some solid object. A hard casing is formed and it turns into a pupa or chrysalis. Great changes take place inside the pupa and at last the fully-formed imago or butterfly (moth) emerges, to mate and start the life cycle again. The butterfly here is the beautiful swallowtail.

Butterflies and moths are quite similar but may be told apart by the 'clubs' at the end of the butterflies' antennae. Butterflies fly by day and sleep with their wings closed over their backs. Most moths are night-fliers.

Eggs can often be found on the underside of leaves. They are small and you must search carefully to find them. Here are the eggs of (1) the swallowtail, (2) Nymphalidae species (such as fritillaries, admirals), (3) Pieridae species (including the 'whites'), (4) Lycaenidae species (the blues and hairstreaks).

Different species of butterfly can vary by tiny details which are easily overlooked. Here are four subspecies of the European meadow brown. All these are females. Individuals of the same species also have variations, sometimes hardly noticeable, at others obvious. In North America the ringlet (also found in Europe) shows similar variations.

The monarch or milkweed undertakes amazing 'wanderings' from its home in America across the Atlantic. It is not uncommon in the Canary Islands, and has occasionally reached the west of Europe, including the British Isles. In the last century it also established itself in Australia and New Zealand.

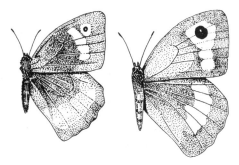

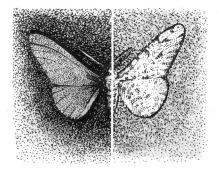

The peppered moth is normally white with a peppering of black, but a dark (melanic) form is becoming common, especially in towns, where their colouring effectively camouflages them on grimy walls or trees. The stick-like caterpillars are of the 'looper' type, arching their bodies as they move.

Moths are far more numerous than butterflies. Their bodies are generally rather thicker and their antennae display a variety of shapes but are never clubbed. You can attract moths at night by painting a branch with honey or some other sweet substance. They are also strongly attracted to bright lights. Their life cycle is the same as butterflies.

Plume moths belong to the Microlepidoptera, a group of small and usually drab moths. The fore and hind wings of plume moths are often deeply split and their long legs are spurred.

Garden tiger-moth caterpillar.

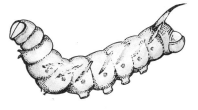

Hawk-moth caterpillar.

The spruce-bud worm (the larva of the moth shown here) is the major pest of North American coniferous forests, burrowing into the centre of the young shoots and destroying them.

Moth caterpillars come in an exciting variety of shapes, colours, size and hairiness. The Microlepidoptera have small, usually insignificant larvae, while hawk-moths have very large, magnificently patterned ones. Some of the hairiest caterpillars, such as the yellow-tail, should be handled with care, as their hairs can cause skin irritation.

Burnets are rather similar to each other. Among the species are the five-spot burnet, the narrow-bordered five-spot burnet and the six-spot burnet. Shown here are the six-spot burnet and a yellow-spotted variety.

The silver-striped hawk-moth shows the typical thick body and narrow fore-wings of its family, and its broken coloration makes it difficult to spot.

17

The Meadow and Hedgerow in Spring

It is an old saying that you can tell when spring has come because you can cover five daisies with your foot. Daisies certainly have a lot to recommend them. The pink-tinged petals are delicate as Lilliputian piano-keys, the stalks are pleasantly sharp-tasting to chew, and one can hardly think of a more time-honoured vernal pastime than sitting on the warm grass and making a daisy chain. But then, there are so many signs of spring that it is delightful to look out for from March to May. I know someone who likes to mention when he has seen the first wild arum (or lords-and-ladies, or jack-in-the-pulpit, or wake-robin: it has different names all over the country). When the plant is fresh and young the 'pulpit', or spathe, is pale green and 'Jack' is a kind of warm purple—a striking sight in a spring hedgerow. Another friend of mine likes to watch for the pink butterbur to come into bloom—a not-so-common early-flowerer that you can hope to find in wet meadows or on the banks of streams from March onwards. Like most less-than-common wild flowers, where you *do* find it, it is usually profuse, and the spikes of pink bloom, growing close together in sheets, cover the ground. My own favourite sign of spring is the brimstone butterfly. Often, in mid or late March, there come a few days of marvellous, heart-stopping weather—warm and sunny, with no wind. (Then it usually turns bitter again—what they call the 'Blackthorn Winter.') During those fine days one often sees brimstones, just out of hibernation, flying along the hedgerows or across the fields. The manner of their flight is very beautiful; as it were, careless and happy. They flutter and glide in the thin, bright air in a way quite different from the drowsy hovering of peacocks or red admirals over the buddleia or lavender bushes of August. Both the fore and the hind wings curve into acute points like rococo decorations, and in the middle of the bright yellow wings are four orange spots—one to each wing. It is as though a cowslip had become a butterfly, fragile and hesitant in the uncertain spring weather, but full of the expectation of summer. These qualities of fragility and a kind of fancied hesitancy characterize other early arrivals—the violets in the banks and the tiny, plume-like, dark-red stamens which shoot from the tips of the hazel buds. These, of course, are the female part of the tree, the male being the catkins with their pollen, which you can shake into a cloud of golden dust in the sunshine.

Stitchwort is common enough, and has no perfume, but I love it simply because it is the whitest flower of any. Most 'white' flowers are not absolutely white when looked at closely. The snowdrop is not really white (it is striped with green and marked with orange too), and neither are the wood anemone, the dead nettle or traveller's joy. But the stitchwort, which comes into bloom up and down the hedges everywhere from April to June, is as pure a white as can be found—as strikingly white as the flashes on the wings of the cock chaffinch. It has one particular relation which is much less common, but well worth looking for. This is a sort of marsh stitchwort, succulent-stemmed like a king-cup, pink and sweetly scented. Its botanical name is *Montia sibirica*, but as far as I know it has no English name yet, not having been very long in this country.

Foxtail grass is good to chew, and so is wild garlic; and wild chives, when they can be found, are perhaps best of all. There is something exciting about hearing the plovers calling by night over ploughed fields where the wheat is beginning to shoot up. Exciting too, by day, to watch the larks soar and fall and run sideways through the grass as they alight; and to hear the green woodpecker laughing all across the fields. Lady's smock, primroses, celandines and wild daffodils—there certainly isn't much to grumble about at this time of year.

Key to Illustration on pages 20-21

ANIMALS

1 Rabbit 2 Lapwing 3 Corn bunting 4 Yellow-hammer 5 Kestrel 6 Skylark 7 Blackbird
8 Grayling (female) 9 Grayling caterpillar 10 Orange-tip (male) 11 Meadow brown (female)
12 Slug 13 Ladybird

PLANTS AND TREES

14 Oak 15 Maple 16 Ash 17 Elm 18 Wheat 19 Rye 20 Hazel 21 Bramble 22 Hawthorn
23 Bindweed 24 Black bryony 25 Ivy 26 Dog-rose 27 Buttercup 28 Meadow saxifrage
29 Green-winged orchid 30 Cowslip 31 Lady's smock 32 Jack-by-the-hedge (garlic mustard)
33 Meadow foxtail 34 Blackthorn 35 Burnet 36 Beech trees 37 Sycamore trees

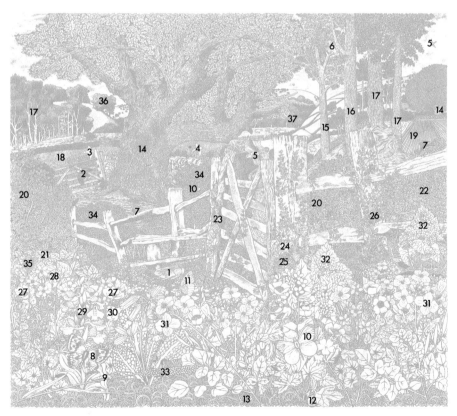

19

The Temperature Switch

In spring, not only do the days get longer but the weather gets warmer. In March it is warmer than in January and in May it is warmer still. But in some years the warmth comes earlier than in others and in these early years flowers also appear earlier. As we have already seen, tulips and daffodils flower earlier if the bulbs are put into a warm cupboard over the cold winter months, and in the same way outdoors an early and warm spring brings on the flowers more quickly.

Hedge garlic, which has all sorts of other country names in England, such as jack-by-the-hedge and garlic mustard, has small white four-petalled flowers and yellowish-green leaves, looking rather like nettle leaves, which smell of garlic when crushed. Usually its flowers appear in April, but if March has been really warm the flowers come out before 1 April and if March is very cold then the flowers may be as much as a week late and not come out before the second week in April.

In countries north of the equator the weather is usually warmer earlier in the south of the country. In England, for instance, it is common to find hedge garlic flowers out as early as the last few days in March in the southern counties, while in the south of Scotland one has to wait until the second or third week in April.

The difference from south to north across a country can be large, but across a continent such as Europe, or to an even greater extent America, the differences are very large indeed. In the south of Europe, spring wheat may come into ear (the flower) in the first week of June and be almost ripe by the end of the month. Near Leningrad on the Baltic coast of Russia, or in Finland, spring wheat does not come into ear until the first week in July and would not be ripe until the end of August. There can even be quite distinct differences between a valley and a hill that are close to each other. If you climb a hill or mountain, the temperature usually drops by about one degree Centigrade for every 165 metres you climb. This is not a very great change in temperature, but it can make a great difference to the growing season, and so in England, in the Pennine hills, which form a sort of backbone to the northern half of England, the shepherds expect lambs in March in the valleys but not until April or even May on the high hills.

In these cases, the increasing warmth acts like the volume knob on a radio; the more the knob is turned up the louder the music or speech becomes, and so with more warmth the plants develop faster. Spring wheat takes only the month of June to ripen its ears at Samarkand or in the southern Ukraine (both in the USSR) where the summers are hot, but at Leningrad it takes most of July and August to ripen.

Spring wheat gets its name because it is sown in the spring. Another kind, sown in the winter, is called winter wheat, and winter wheat not only responds to increasing warmth (like turning up the volume switch on the radio) but also has to be switched on. The switch in this case is the intense cold of winter; if you sowed winter wheat in a bowl and put it in a warm cupboard, as we did with the daffodils and tulips, it would not flower, however warm the cupboard. It must grow where it can feel the cold of winter. Many plants have to be switched on by the cold of winter. A cousin of the wood meadow-grass, called simply the blue grass, is one of these. Even if you grew this grass throughout winter in a heated greenhouse it

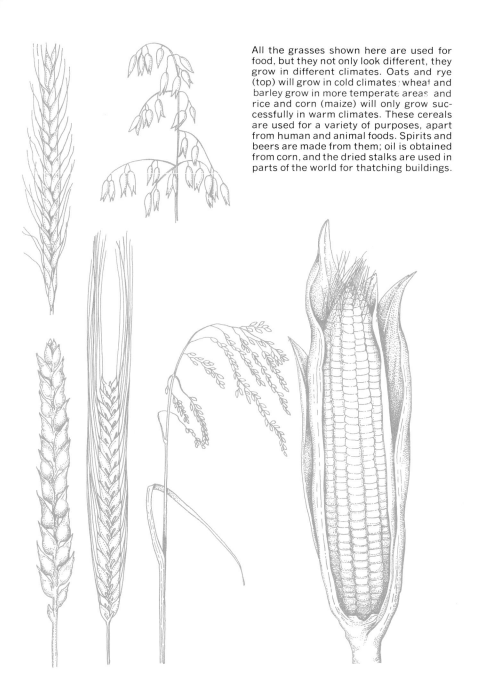

All the grasses shown here are used for food, but they not only look different, they grow in different climates. Oats and rye (top) will grow in cold climates; wheat and barley grow in more temperate areas and rice and corn (maize) will only grow successfully in warm climates. These cereals are used for a variety of purposes, apart from human and animal foods. Spirits and beers are made from them; oil is obtained from corn, and the dried stalks are used in parts of the world for thatching buildings.

would not flower, though its leaves would get very long. This grass is a *perennial* plant, which grows for many years, but the biggest group of plants that need the cold of winter to switch them on are the *biennials*, which germinate (sprout), grow and lay down stores of food in the first year but do not flower until the second year. The parsnips in the vegetable garden or in the greengrocer, the sugar beet in the farmers' fields, cow parsley, chervil in the hedge banks and roadsides, the wild celery in the ditches and hemlock on waste ground and riversides are all biennials which need the cold of winter to make them flower in the following year. They all need cold to switch them on and warmth to make them grow.

23

Seedeater
Redpolls have stout beaks, typical of seed-eaters. Their food in summer consists mainly of grain, and sorrel, spruce and chickweed seeds and a few insects and larvae. In winter they eat birch and alder seeds, birch catkins and mountain ash (rowan) berries.

Birds have developed a variety of beak shapes to fit their environment and feeding habits. Here are a few examples.

Insectivore
The wren's diet is mainly small insects and their larvae, spiders and a few seeds. The narrow bill enables it to pick its diet out of small cracks.

Carnivore
Like other hawks and predators, the kestrel has a powerful hooked beak for tearing at flesh, and powerful talons for catching and gripping its prey. Its chief food is mice, grasshoppers, beetles and caterpillars. It takes very few birds.

24

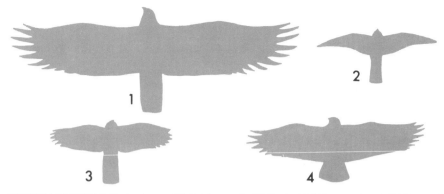

BIRD SILHOUETTES Birds of prey: (1) Golden eagle (2) Kestrel (3) Sparrowhawk (4) Buzzard

The male teal (1a) is a very brightly marked little duck, while his mate (1b) is a drab mottled brown and buff. This enables her to remain inconspicuous on the nest, while the male's rich colours attract her at breeding time. The water rail, on the other hand, is similar in both sexes, though the male (2a) has stronger markings.

BIRD SILHOUETTES Water birds: (1) Grey heron (2) Mallard (3) Bean goose (4) Red-throated diver (5) Whooper swan

25

The Lake and Stream in Spring

Dear water, clear water, playful in all your streams,
As you dash or loiter through life who does not love
To sit beside you?

These lines of W. H. Auden express perfectly, for me, what most of us feel about streams. Running water is necessary to our life, of course— we *have* to drink it, use it for washing and so on—but we *think* of it, in our hearts, as the best of all playthings, and particularly when we are children. The little Enborne brook, the county boundary between Berkshire and Hampshire, must be typical of thousands of streams with which children have always played, everywhere. In one place on its banks, many years ago, a pine tree tilted and half-fell, sloping across one of the deeper pools, and here boys used to bathe, plunging in off the crusty, bark-flaking trunk and pulling themselves out by the tough, flexible branches. Further up, along an open reach, low alder bushes lined the bank, covered, in spring, with their long, purplish catkins and hard, round, nut-like flower buds. A cheap muslin fishing-net on a bamboo stick brought up marvellous creatures from the bed of the stream—kicking, scurrying water-shrimps, the fantastic stick-houses of frail caddis worms, perhaps a water boatman or two, jerking along with their oar-like legs, and sinister, elastic leeches, stretching themselves out and drawing themselves in as they traversed smoothly the glass side of the jam-jar. One day a 'real little fish'—a minnow— came up in the net. I remember well the moment when I realized, with a shock of wonder, that every pond, every little stream, was a teeming, subaqueous world, as vast, populous and self-contained as our own world above.

Streams, of course, have their own kinds of local plants, flowers and trees. Best of all these, surely, are the kingcups, which bloom in great sheets of gold, in marshy places, in March and April. Later in spring— not much before May—come the ragged robins (they are campions) with their beautiful, segmented petals, looking not ragged at all, but more like a girl in some exquisite and fantastic fancy-dress. The water-cress comes into flower in May, too, but it can be picked and eaten well before that—at any time of year, in fact; but the spring shoots are the best. It is found only in clear, running water, and its peppery, crisp taste goes particularly well with toast and potted meat. Cuckoo flowers are in bloom along the wet banks by April, and the willow catkins start coming out: big, soft, furry catkins they are, too. *Salix fragilis,* the crack willow, is a particularly pretty one.

Kingfishers like to make a tunnel in a sandy or soft earth bank a foot or two above the stream—unless they are lucky enough to find one already made or to be able to make use of an old site of their own—and at the far end of this they make their nest. One can often stand unobserved and watch the cock bird coming and going with food and hear the young ones squeaking with excitement as he disappears down the hole, minnow in beak. The brilliant, cobalt kingfisher is certainly the most striking of all British river birds; but two others well worth watching for are the dipper and the grey wagtail. The dipper is very neat— a tubby, fussy, little black-and-white bird. The cock grey wagtail is noticeably yellow beneath, as well as grey above, and one can hope to see him strutting and bobbing (in behaviour exactly like the commoner 'pied wagtail') on the sill of a weir, on a plank bridge, or any point of vantage just above the water.

Key to Illustration on pages 28-29

ANIMALS

1 Swallow 2 Heron 3 Mute swan and cygnets 4 Pied wagtail 5 Reed bunting 6 Kingfisher 7 Grey wagtail 8 Skylark 9 Coot 10 Mallard (male) 11 Mallard (female)

PLANTS AND TREES

12 Willow (pollarded) 13 Alders 14 Oak 15 Hawthorn 16 Reedmace (bulrush) 17 Reeds 18 Bur-reed 19 Marsh stitchwort 20 Common watercress 21 Water violet 22 Brooklime 23 Lesser spearwort 24 Ragged robin 25 Marsh violet 26 Rushes 27 Coot's nest 28 Reed sweet-grass 29 Annual meadow-grass 30 Common cat's-tail grass 31 Common spike-rush

Animal Display

Along the stream, both under the water and above it, animals behave differently as the weather gets hotter and the days get longer. As with the plants in the meadow and the wood, the longer days and higher temperatures switch on animal activity again. For example, sticklebacks (or tittlebats, as some people call them) can usually be seen in shoals, or schools, but in spring the males leave the schools and pick a part of the stream which they fiercely defend as if it was their very own piece of water. When another fish, especially if it is another male stickleback, comes near, the 'owner' will rush toward the stranger and warn him off. By spring he is a very fine-looking fellow, with a greenish back, a red belly and blue eyes, and as he charges the intruder his spines stick up and his mouth opens, as though he is going to bite. Often this bold display is enough to send the stranger on his way. Yet if the stranger stands his ground, the stickleback does not actually attack him—he merely stands on his head and jerks about as if he wanted to attack the bottom of the stream!

When he is not driving off trespassers, the male, or cock, stickleback builds a nest by scooping a shallow bowl out of the bed of the stream and pressing small water plants down into it. He glues these plants together with a liquid which comes from his kidneys until he has constructed a tunnel only just wider than his own body. After building his nest his colours become even more bright and he swaggers round his territory, hoping to attract a female to his nest. Once this has happened, he goes on looking after the nest and fans his tail to send a flow of fresh water over the eggs. He is a good father, and when the young hatch out he looks after them. If one of them tries to swim away he chases after it, catches it in his mouth and spits it out among its brothers and sisters.

But as his offspring grow older and bolder, he begins to lose interest and they eventually join a school of their own age.

High above the stream a skylark spirals up and up. His flight perhaps wanders slightly, for he, like the stickleback, is defining the territory that he will hold during the breeding period. During the breeding season he is held to this territory and hovers above it like a kite on a string. You can first watch him doing this in February, and despite the winds that might blow him away, he will always manage to stay over the same small area of ground.

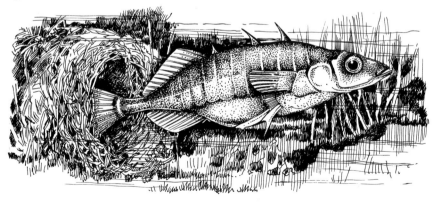

The male three-spined stickleback, resplendent in courting colours, patrols outside his nest hoping to attract the attention of a passing female.

Courting great crested grebes have an elaborate ritual during which both partners present each other with nesting materials.

But what are the singing skylark and the brightly coloured stickleback really doing? Their antics have several purposes. By keeping a small territory for themselves they spread the number of birds and fishes over a wide area, so that there is enough food for all the families. Their attractive songs, colour and behaviour will help to draw the female to them and stimulate her to lay eggs and may also act as a trigger to put fear into a rival male or feelings of love in a female.

But the female must also trigger a friendly reception in the male. For instance, when the female stickleback is ready to lay eggs, she swims with her head up and her tail down, which is a definite signal to the male to fertilize the eggs.

Animals use all sorts of ways to produce these trigger reactions which are used to help courtship move to a successful conclusion. The goldfinch postures and shows his brilliant wings to the female, and mallard and garganey drakes preen themselves to show off their brightest plumage. The male and female great crested grebes have a more active set of movements and present nesting material to each other in an elaborate display.

But watch the animals carefully. Not all colour patterns, for instance, are aids to courtship. When the bobbing white tail of the rabbit appears, it means 'run for cover'!

Reptiles and Amphibians

Frogs, toads and newts are all amphibians —animals that must return to water to breed and which, as fish-like tadpoles or newt larvae, actually live under water and breathe by means of gills. These tadpoles or larvae hatch from eggs and later change their shape, grow limbs, lose their gills and 'metamorphose' into small adults.

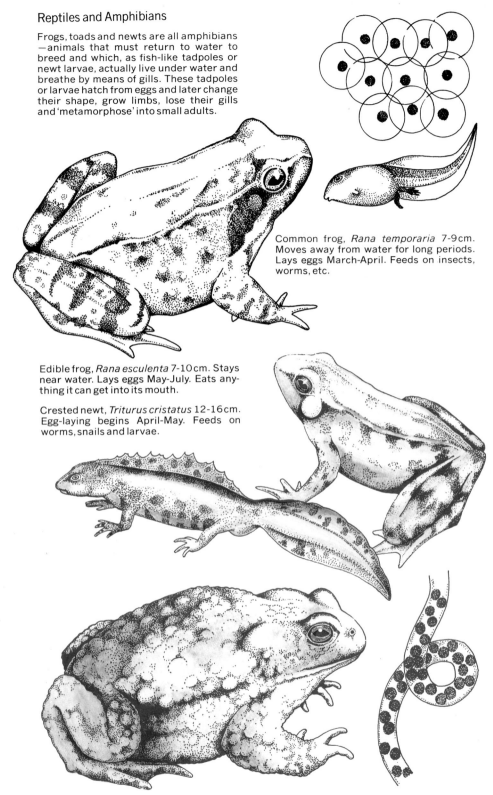

Common frog, *Rana temporaria* 7-9 cm. Moves away from water for long periods. Lays eggs March-April. Feeds on insects, worms, etc.

Edible frog, *Rana esculenta* 7-10 cm. Stays near water. Lays eggs May-July. Eats anything it can get into its mouth.

Crested newt, *Triturus cristatus* 12-16 cm. Egg-laying begins April-May. Feeds on worms, snails and larvae.

Common toad, *Bufo bufo* 8-12 cm. Lays eggs May-June. Feeds on worms, slugs, insects, etc.

Eggs of common toad are laid in a string of 5000-7000. These hatch after 8-10 days.

Snakes are reptiles, but they have no limbs. When they emerge from hibernation, usually in April, they may cast off their skins, or 'slough'. Sloughing then takes place about once every month until the snakes go into hibernation again in the autumn. (Dangerous snakes are marked with a red dot beside the illustration.)

Lizards are also reptiles. Most of them have limbs. They usually lay eggs. If caught, lizards, especially slow-worms, shed their tails, which they can then re-grow.

Viviparous (common lizard), *Lacerta vivipara* Up to 18cm long. Damp meadows and moorland. Main food earthworms, insects and larvae.

Adder (or European viper), *Vipera berus* 50-60cm long. Dry sunny places. Feeds on mice, lizards, slow-worms, frogs. Poisonous bite.

Slow-worms, *Anguis fragilis* Up to 50cm long. Damp shady places. Main food earthworms.

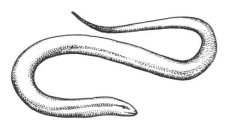

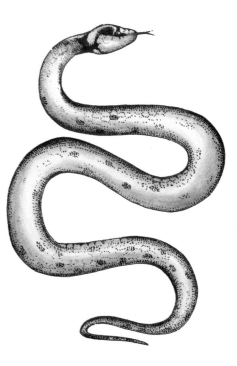

HOW TO TELL SNAKES APART

Adders have thick-set bodies, a flat broad head, at the back of which is usually a dark X or V marking. They have a zig-zag pattern down the middle of their backs. Males are pale grey, with black markings; females and young brownish with paler markings.

Grass snakes have long slender bodies and half-moon-shaped markings on the collar. There are usually blueish bar markings down the length of the body.

Smooth snakes, which are much rarer, are slender with smooth and shining scales. A dark line runs through their eye to the corner of the mouth. The back has a double row of oblong spots. The smooth snake kills by constricting its prey in its coils and then eating it before it is dead.

Grass snake, *Natrix natrix* Male up to 100cm, female up to 150cm long. Usually lives near water. Main food frogs.

33

The Wood in Summer

May and June are the great time for bird-song—in England, anyway. Deep woodland—that is, thick trees—is not attractive to many birds except the nightingale; but the edges of woods, or an open copse— one that has been recently thinned out, for instance—these they love and frequent. I like to get up very early on a June morning—it gets light about quarter past four—and wander quietly about, listening to the birds, for they sing best at dawn and evening and at dawn there is less interruption from human noise. The ones that give me most pleasure are the warblers—migrants who arrive in April or early May and sing little, if at all, after midsummer. The blackcap is a beautiful songster, but better still, to my way of thinking, is the garden warbler. His pitch is lower than the blackcap's and he sustains his song for longer. Then there is always a chance, if one is up early, of seeing (and hearing) the cuckoo at close quarters, though usually it will be because he happens to pass close to you rather than because you succeed in getting close to him. Cuckoos are shy birds; yet only last year, on a May morning, one flew close above my head, calling (for they call mostly on the wing). How many people, I wonder, have been made happy by hearing the cuckoo on a fine morning in early summer? There isn't a country in Europe that hasn't got at least one folk song about the cuckoo. It could almost be called an important part of the human heritage, but perhaps old words are better, 'She bringeth us good tidings, she telleth us no lies.'

It may not be altogether easy to learn to recognize the songs of the warblers—though for the matter of that, it is not terribly difficult, and for the pleasure they give, it is well worth while—but anyone can stand and watch the thrush or the blackbird singing. If blackbirds were rare, people would come hundreds of miles to them. Too many are killed by cars every summer, for they are slow flyers and often tired, I think, towards the end of a summer's day. It is long, hard work foraging for yourself, a hen and a brood of nestlings as well. The death of the cock condemns the whole family, unless the nestlings are ready to fly, so for anyone who is driving a car, it is always worth remembering to go slowly and watchfully up leafy lanes in summer. Blackbirds have no rights at law—but all the same I seem to remember something about not one sparrow falling to the ground unobserved.

Honeysuckle, too, likes the edges of woods, although when you find one, you will often discover that it is rooted six or ten feet back inside the wood, and that the sprays have come trailing out. That honeysuckle knows what it is about, for in late summer, when everything is hot and dry, the ground is likely to be still damp in the wood, so that the roots will be in the green shade, along with other shade-loving flowers of late summer—sanicles, archangels and yellow pimpernels, for instance. The high summer, as they call late July and

August, is often the best time to enjoy woodland, for then it is cool and shady when everything outside has turned dry and brown. In a heat wave, one always feels at least a little cooler under a beech tree.

In summer when the shaws be sheen
And leaves be large and long,
Full merry it is in fair forest
To hear the fowlés song.

That's about five hundred years old—and, as they say in Berkshire, 'I dunno as I can do 'ny better.'

Key to Illustration on pages 36-37

ANIMALS

1 Hawfinch 2 Great-spotted woodpecker 3 Long-tailed tit 4 Common blue
5 Small tortoiseshell 6 Small copper 7 Wood white

PLANTS AND TREES

8 Wych elm 9 Ash 10 Oak 11 Maple 12 Beech 13 Silver birch 14 Sessile oak 15 Rowan
16 Elm 17 Sycamore 18 Small-leaved lime 19 Tree stump of oak 20 Tree stump of elm
21 Saint John's wort 22 Common forget-me-not 23 Enchanter's nightshade 24 Ivy
25 Red campion 26 Butterfly orchid 27 Columbine 28 Common violet 29 Hawthorn
30 Hazel 31 Bracken 32 Destroying angel 33 Holly

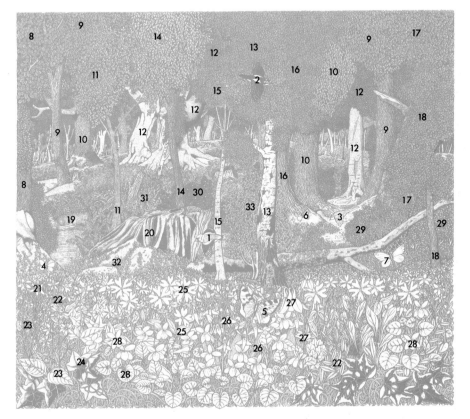

Food and Energy

We all need food to give us the energy to do things. Plants also need energy to grow, and they too need to feed, though only a few (mostly those that trap and digest insects) can actually be seen eating.

The main source of energy for plants comes from the light of the sun. You can prove this by growing peas in pots, some in the sunlight and some in dark cupboards. All the peas will grow at first because they are living on food stored in the actual pea seed and the ones in the dark cupboard will probably grow taller and faster because they are trying to reach the light. But if the cupboard is really dark the peas in it will die when they have used up their store of food. The peas in the light, on the other hand, will go on growing because their green leaves trap the energy of the sunlight. They then use this trapped energy to make food, such as sugar and other *carbohydrates* as they are called, oils and proteins. This food gives the plants, and incidentally any animals which eat them, the energy to grow and reproduce, and in the case of the animals the energy to hunt and move.

Some plants are able to store a lot of food to give them a good start in the spring. Flowers like the bluebell and jack-in-the-pulpit or lords-and-ladies store food in bulbs and tubers beneath the ground. Early in the spring, before the trees grow their leaves and shut out most of the sunlight, they grow their own new leaves to capture the sun's energy. In other plants, such as the winter aconite, which grows in southern Europe and can often be seen in gardens in England, most of the stored food is used to produce flowers first and the leaves come later.

Deciduous trees allow more light to reach the ground in spring. This means they trap less energy and so grow less quickly than coniferous trees. Those shown here are (top) beech and oak; and (below) sycamore and elm.

The conifers are (top) yew and larch; and (below) Sitka spruce, Scots pine and Douglas fir.

In countries where the sun shines all year, the trapping of energy and storing of food is not linked to bright summer days and to dull winter ones but to the wet and dry seasons.

In the northern part of the world the season of bright summer days is very short and the sky is often cloudy, so woodland trees have found another way of capturing the sun's energy. They keep their leaves all the year round so that they can catch even the weak winter sun and trap its energy. These 'evergreen' trees often grow in a different way too. A wood of evergreen trees, such as pines and most firs, appears spiky, while a wood of deciduous trees (trees which drop their leaves in winter) has a much flatter top.

Which type of tree is best at catching the sun's energy? Go into a pine wood and see how dark it is. Then go into an oak wood and you will see that a lot of light filters through the leaves and reaches the ground. The pine wood traps nearly all the sun's light and the floor of a pine wood has very few green plants, but the floor of an oak wood is rich with many different kinds of plants and low undergrowth.

Because the evergreen trees are better at catching light than oak or ash trees they grow faster. This is why trees such as pines are so commonly grown for timber, though their fast growth produces a softer wood than oak or ash.

Animal Life in an Oak Tree

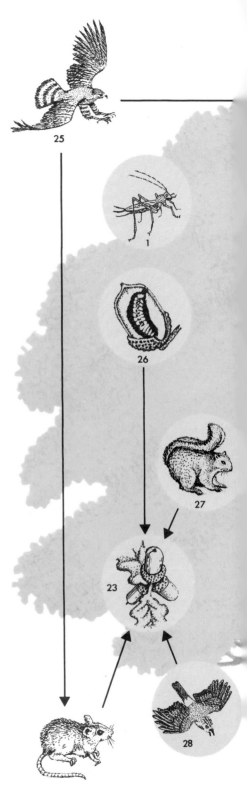

An oak tree is a good place to observe the interdependence of animal and plant life. Leaves, bark, acorns, roots are eaten or attacked by a variety of animals. Many of these animals are themselves the prey of other animals. As they die, or are passed out of animals' bodies as droppings, they are broken down by bacteria and returned to the earth.

The diagram shows, by arrows, which animals feed on which other animals. The key tells briefly what each does.

1 The bush cricket feeds at the top of the tree.
2 Coal tits feed on a variety of insects.
3 Hairstreak caterpillars feed on the leaves.
4 Dunbar-moth caterpillars feed both on the leaves and on other caterpillars.
5 Winter-moth caterpillars are a food for many other animals.
6 The larvae of ichneumonid wasps, parasitize caterpillars.
7 The larvae of tachinid flies also parasitize caterpillars.
8 Leaf weevil larvae are leaf miners.
9, 10, 11 Mirid bugs feed on flowers and young leaves. One of them, *Miris striatus*, is also a general predator.
12 Braconid-wasp larvae are parasites on mirid bugs.
13 Scale insects feed on young stems and form pit galls.
14 Oak aphids suck the undersides of leaves.
15 Leafhoppers feed on leaves.
16 Hunting spiders lurk among the leaves.
17 Oak-bark beetles eat the bark and breed under it.
18, 19 The gall wasp forms currant and spangle galls in alternate generations.
20, 21 Other gall wasps form oak-apple and root galls.
22 Some braconid wasps are parasites on gall wasps.
23 Acorns are food for several animals.
24 Wood mice feed on acorns and are the prey of sparrowhawks.
25 The sparrowhawk preys on mice and birds.
26 The larvae of the nut weevil live in acorns.
27 Grey squirrels feed on acorns.
28 The jay also feeds on acorns.

The Meadow and Hedgerow in Summer

There is a stillness about the meadows in the hot days of summer, as though the year were poised motionless at the top of a long slope up which it has climbed and from which it must later descend—but not yet, thank goodness. The cows stand all together in the shadiest place they can find, swishing their tails to keep off the horseflies; the deep-blue sky seems closer above the trees than in spring, and in the drowsy afternoon the only sound is the murmurous, monotonous call of a wood pigeon, warm and unhurried as the day itself. If the field is on the slopes of the Downs, the dry, hollow cloppering of a sheep-bell may perhaps be heard as the flock grazes over the turf; and everywhere drifts the sweet, chrysanthemum-like smell of the Compositae—the daisy family plants of high summer: the tansy, ragwort and corn—chamomile, the yarrow and mugwort. The big purple-headed thistles have the most beautiful perfume. No doubt this is why one so often finds a bumble-bee sitting drowsily in the middle of the bloom.

Some of the best wild flowers of all are to be found on the Downs and in the upland meadows in high summer. The chicory, with a stem so tough that it is a hard job to pick it, has scentless, pale-blue blooms, finely fronded in the centre, their petals serrated along the outer edges. The milkwort creeps through the grass, and seems almost to be hiding its little, deep-blue flowers, with their two upper petals spread like wings. Along the dry hedgerows there will be tall plants of viper's bugloss—not that I ever saw a viper anywhere near one—or 'Joseph-and-Mary,' as it is sometimes called, on account of the flower being red in bud and blue in full bloom. Both colours appear together, for the spike of the plant comes into bloom from the foot upwards, with red buds at the top and blue flowers lower down—a striking sight. The mullein must be the tallest wild flower of all—taller than the foxglove—with its thick, velvet-soft leaves and yellow spike of bloom sometimes rising higher than a man's head.

The ragwort is often covered with the yellow and black caterpillars of the cinnabar moth, and it is not so difficult to find the moth herself—a frail, fluttering, drowsy creature, with a black body and wings of brilliant cerise and near-black. The chalk blue, too, will be fanning its wings and flitting among the harebells and long grass, and perhaps the tortoiseshell and the orange tip as well. Down in the grass, the insects clamber and scurry through the hot days. Many have no names, for there are thousands of different kinds of insects and not all have been classified. As evening falls, great cockchafers come droning by in the cooling air and often, if one stands still and watches the wasps going home, one can follow them to their nest in hedgerow or bank, for they work entirely by instinct and cannot mislead or deceive you. (But they can sting you all right if you interfere with their nest; and very painful it is.)

The marvellous colours of the sunset fade, the huge moon rises, the owls begin to call as they set out and the little grasshopper warbler sets up his whickering call down the meadow. Life could never be long enough to hold all the summer evenings one would like to enjoy.

Key to illustration on pages 44-45

ANIMALS

1 Fox 2 Redwing 3 Wood pigeon 4 Magpie 5 Chaffinch 6 Linnet 7 Crows 8 Brimstone 9 Small copper 10 Small tortoiseshell 11 Adonis blue

PLANTS AND TREES

12 Oak 13 Maple 14 Ash 15 Elm 16 Wheat 17 Hazel 18 Bramble 19 Blackthorn 20 Hawthorn 21 Bindweed 22 Black bryony 23 Dog rose 24 Ivy 25 Rye 26 Larkspur 27 Buttercup 28 Meadow saxifrage 29 Greater stitchwort 30 Harebell 31 Herb robert 32 Yellow chamomile 33 Corn chamomile 34 Creeping cinquefoil 35 Persian speedwell 36 Common yellow rocket 37 Old man's beard 38 Cow parsley 39 Charlock 40 Chervil 41 Scarlet pimpernel 42 Field mouse-ear 43 Beech trees 44 Shepherd's purse

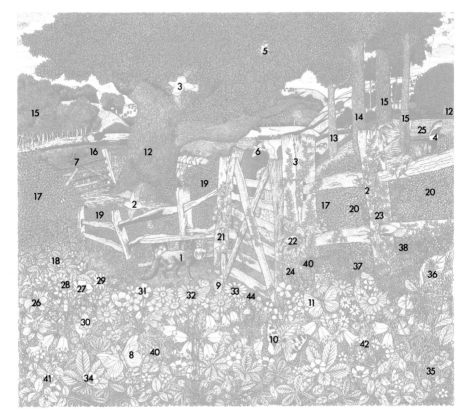

Pollination

To produce fertile seeds a plant usually needs pollen from the stamen to be brought into contact with the stigma so that the ovary can be fertilized. The stigma is part of the female organs of a plant and the stamen part of the male organs. Plants have several ways in which this contact can be brought about and their flowers are differently shaped and arranged so that pollination, as it is called, can best be brought about. The two most common methods of pollination are by wind and by insect.

Wind-pollinated plants, which include many trees, shrubs and herbs with rather uninteresting flowers, such as oaks, hazel, grasses and plantains, have large stamens which dangle on long stalks, often in hanging catkins. In this way the wind can easily shake them and knock the pollen into the air. The stigmas are also large and often look rather like feathers, so that their feathery edges can trap the pollen as it blows along on the breeze. Petals and other parts which we usually think of as being the most obvious characteristics of a flower are very small or are even not there at all. This allows the stamens and stigmas to have every chance to do their important work. And with these wind-pollinated flowers the stamens and stigmas are usually in different flowers, which prevents a stigma being covered with pollen from the next-door stamen. If this should happen then any weakness in a plant might become worse when its seeds germinated.

Plants produce pollen at different times of the year. Most trees, such as hazel, elm and alder, produce pollen in March, though willow and ash are ready later, in April. In the meadow the low plants, such as grasses, flower in June, but the common nettle goes on producing pollen from June to September.

While the wind-pollinated flowers are rather dull to look at, insect-pollinated flowers are often very beautiful and have striking markings on them which guide the insects to the nectar on which they feed. Some, like the snapdragon, have platforms on which the insect can land, and in insect-pollinated flowers there is always some mechanism which makes sure that the pollen brushes off on the insect as it feeds. Then when it settles on another plant of the same species or kind it brushes the pollen off its body on to the stigmas of the new plant. The pollen then passes down the tube of the stigma and fertilizes the ovary where the 'eggs' are stored and these eventually become seeds.

The colours and the patterns on flowers which attract insects are fascinating. Some have dark lines (*pollen guides*) which guide the insects towards the hidden nectar. Others, like the meadow buttercup, appear to be a brilliant shining yellow, because on the petals there is an upper layer of oily yellow colouring under which lies a layer of starch grains which reflects the light back through the upper layer of yellow, giving the buttercup that brilliant yellow which is so strong that it will reflect its colour on your skin on a bright day.

Many insects visit flowers for the sweet nectar, but pollen is itself a food for many insects. The nectar is made in special parts of the flowers called nectaries. They can easily be seen in buttercups, but very often the petals join to make a long tube with the nectaries at the bottom. Then the insects have to push down the tube past the stamens and stigma to get to the sweet nectar. This ensures that the pollen gets brushed off on the

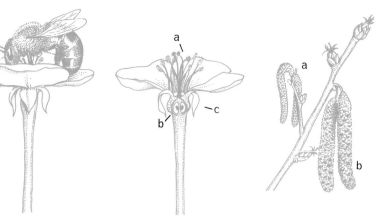

Pollination of the apple is of the simplest kind. The visiting insect, seeking nectar, picks up pollen on its body and transfers it to another flower.
(a) Anther, (b) Concave receptacle enclosing pistil, (c) Sepals.

The hanging male catkins of the silver birch are swayed by the wind, which blows their pollen on to the small stigmas of the female catkins.
(a) Female, (b) Male.

insect which then will transfer it to a stigma. Campions and cowslips have these tubes, and so does the primrose under the hedge and the honeysuckle in the hedge itself.

On the other hand, colours do have a very important part to play in attracting the insects to pollinate them. Different colours attract different insects even in the same group. Amongst butterflies the tortoiseshells like yellow or blue flowers, but take no notice of those which are green or blue-green. The large white shows a strong preference for blues, purple and violets, but ignores yellow or orange.

Bees cannot see red, but it can be shown that they can tell the difference between yellow, blue and blue-green. They are also sensitive to ultraviolet, which we cannot see, and so some flowers that look the same colour to us are quite different to bees. The cinquefoil and primula both have yellow flowers, but bees see the first one as purple. And forget-me-not and speedwell are both blue to us while the bee sees the speedwell as violet.

Because bees are sensitive to ultraviolet, they can see things that we cannot see, even though they are red-blind. Look around and you will see how many flowers have spots and stripes—perhaps a third of all the flowers you see—but for a bee, because it sees the ultraviolet light waves, perhaps two-thirds of all flowers have spots or stripes.

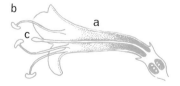

Honeysuckle is pollinated by bumble bees and some moths. Their long tongues seek the nectar at the base of the long corolla (a) and in doing so brush the pollen off the anthers (b) on to the stigmas (c). The pollen then travels down the style to fertilize the eggs in the ovary.

In both the bee orchid and the green-winged orchid, the flowers can be fertilized by visiting insects on whose bodies the *pollinia* (clinging masses of pollen grains) stick, but in the case of the bee orchid the pollinia *usually* fall on to the stigma, so that they are self-pollinated, and do not need visiting insects.

47

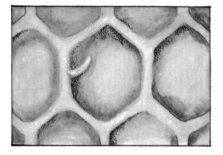

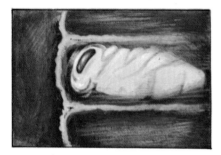
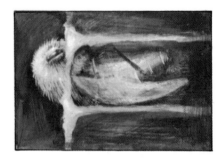

The Life of the Honey Bee

Honey bees live in well-organized hives, made up from a series of combs. The combs are built of wax secreted by workers and consist of six-sided cells placed back to back. Some combs are used for rearing the young, others for storing honey or pollen for food. The queen may lay up to 2000 eggs a day and one is placed in each of the breeding cells. This develops into a white larva which in turn changes into a horny pupa and eventually hatches as the adult bee. The larvae are at first fed on royal jelly, made from special glands on the workers. One larva is singled out to be the new queen and this is fed on royal jelly until it is fully developed — 16 days from hatching. The queen larva has a specially large cell constructed for her.

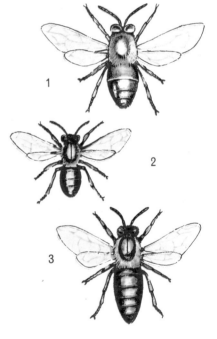

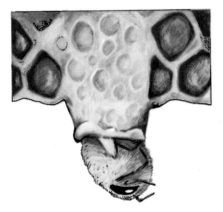

There are three types of bee in each hive — one queen (1), workers (2) and drones (3). The great majority in a hive are workers. These are sterile females and are the smallest bees in the hives. They build the hives, collect food and feed the young. The drones are males. They are larger and stouter with bigger eyes. The queen is the only fertile female. She has a longer abdomen than the others, which extends beyond her closed wings.

When the workers set out to collect pollen and nectar (which they later regurgitate in the form of honey) they perform the important job of pollinating the flowers they visit. Pollen is collected in sacs on their legs, and as the worker pushes through the petals to obtain the nectar at the base of the flower, pollen caught from the anthers of one plant rubs off on the stigma of another.

The cells are neatly glued together by the sticky gum from horse chestnut (below) or other buds. This gum is also used to 'mummify' foreign objects in the hive such as a stray beetle.

When workers return to the hive from their food collecting they perform complicated dances. These communicate to other bees the direction and distance of the food flowers, the relative quantity of food available and the type of plant to be found.

A flourishing hive may have as many as 80,000 bees. Once a year, when the new queen is fully grown, the old queen flies out pursued by a huge swarm of workers. These swarms may be seen on a summer's day darkening the air or clinging in a great crawling ball on a branch.

Eventually a site is found for a new hive. Meanwhile, the new queen in the old hive flies out for her marriage flight pursued by eager male drones and she is fertilized in mid-air before returning to the hive.

The Lake and Stream in Summer

In July and August, the fields and hills often seem hushed—almost arid—in the heat. Greenness turns parched or brown and only the yellowhammer twitters in the hot afternoon. But by the river there is no such stillness. This is the river's bountiful, luxuriant time. Along the banks, great clumps of flowering plants spring up and bloom like a herbaceous border—purple loosestrife, the yellow daisies of the fleabane, fluffy, pink, hemp agrimony, great willow herb, the huge white whorls of the great water dock, and dark-red, tough, square-stemmed figwort (which is pollinated almost only by wasps). They make fine cover for the fisherman to stalk a rising trout. In the water itself—in the stiller reaches—other, fantastic plants are in bloom: the yellow water lily, its long stalks trailing deep—sometimes several feet to the bed of the river. This is the lily called 'brandy-bottle', from the shape of the big, green seed-pod when the flower is over. Close by there may be arrowhead (so-called from the shape of the leaves rising clear out of the water), with its white, purple-eyed flowers branching out of the main stalk in little clusters. The flowering rush likes still water, and here it puts up its head of frail, deep-pink blooms (three big petals alternating with three small ones) on a stalk which is often as much as three feet tall. The crowfoots (or crowfeet?), of which there are many, are water buttercups, though their flowers are white and their leaves submerged; and the hornwort and mare's tail (which are more likely to be found in canals, perhaps, than in rivers) have a strangely old, prehistoric look, as though they once grew in dinosaurs' swamps long ago.

Unexpected things may happen by a river in time of drought. One hot August afternoon, many years ago, a certain fisherman was working conscientiously through the inactive time of the day. (Trout rise best at morning and evening.) Coming to a wide bed of tall reeds, he saw that some fairly big animal was moving in there; and a moment later a badger, whom the heat must have driven down to drink in broad daylight, pushed its way out and lumbered off up the slope to the near-by woods. Another day that same fisherman, working up a side-stream, came upon a swimming otter, which pulled itself out and bounded away, with a lithe leaping, across the water-meadow.

During the earlier part of the summer, the heron is a hard worker, and as long as he is undisturbed will often stab and paddle away in the running shallows for hours, coming and going to his nestlings with slow, heavy beats of his grey wings. In contrast is the dashing speed of the swifts and swallows, which seems to fill the whole river with movement as they turn and flash, hunting flies over the water; or break the surface for an instant (either sipping, or snatching a floating fly) before racing up and away. In the sedge hover the great dragonflies (four-engined dragonflies, we used to call them), green, and ochre, and glittering blue, with their great, panelled eyes and segmented bodies.

50

Like hummingbirds, they hold themselves poised in the air, vanish as they dart away in a split second and then resume their tense stillness a few yards along the bank. In a shallow pool under the bank a great pike, two feet long, basks and dozes in the warm water. The water-mint has a sleepy smell; but if we are asleep, it is a sleep like Caliban's. When we wake, we cry to dream again.

Key to Illustration on pages 52-53

ANIMALS

1 Heron 2 Swift 3 Mute swan and cygnets 4 Sand martin 5 Kingfisher 6 Reed bunting
7 Swallow 8 Shoveler (male) 9 Shoveler (female) 10 Mallard (male) 11 Mallard (female)
12 Dragonfly (male) 13 Grey wagtail 14 Moorhen 15 Teal (male) 16 Teal (female)
17 Young pochards 18 Coot

TREES AND PLANTS

19 Oak 20 Willow (pollarded) 21 Alders 22 Hawthorn 23 Reedmace (bulrush) 24 Reeds
25 Bur-reed 26 Arrowhead 27 Brooklime 28 Yellow water lily 29 River crowfoot
30 Water-violet 31 Marsh willow herb 32 Common watercress 33 Waterwort
34 Great water forget-me-not.

Animal Dispersion

You have already read about the light and temperature switches which turn plants and animals on or off, and of the antics of the male stickleback which 'turns on' the female in spring and the danger signal which the bobbing white tail of the rabbit gives. But these are not the only messages passed and received by animals. The stickleback, for example, defends his territory, when another male comes too close, by appearing to attack him. But as we have seen he does not carry out his attack to the bitter end. He does his 'headstand'. Why is this? Presumably because the intruder nearly always swims away. But then *why* does the intruder swim away? Scientists think that it is because by not engaging in battle the species benefits, for not only does neither male get hurt, but the defending male stickleback can look after his small piece of stream bed and raise his family in peace, with enough water surrounding him (his territory) to enable him to get all the food needed to feed him, his mate and his family. Sticklebacks when breeding can thus become quite equally spaced over all the available stream bed.

But now let's think about the coot swimming on the surface. In the nesting season coots become very aggressive and jealously guard their own pond or stretch of the stream against possible rivals. It does not matter if the pond is tiny or if it is quite a lake—their ferocity ensures that no other coots nest near them on their pond.

But if a pair of coots are so successful on a small pond, are they really using their territory well? Since one pair only produces a few eggs each season, being aggressive must mean that fewer young birds can be born

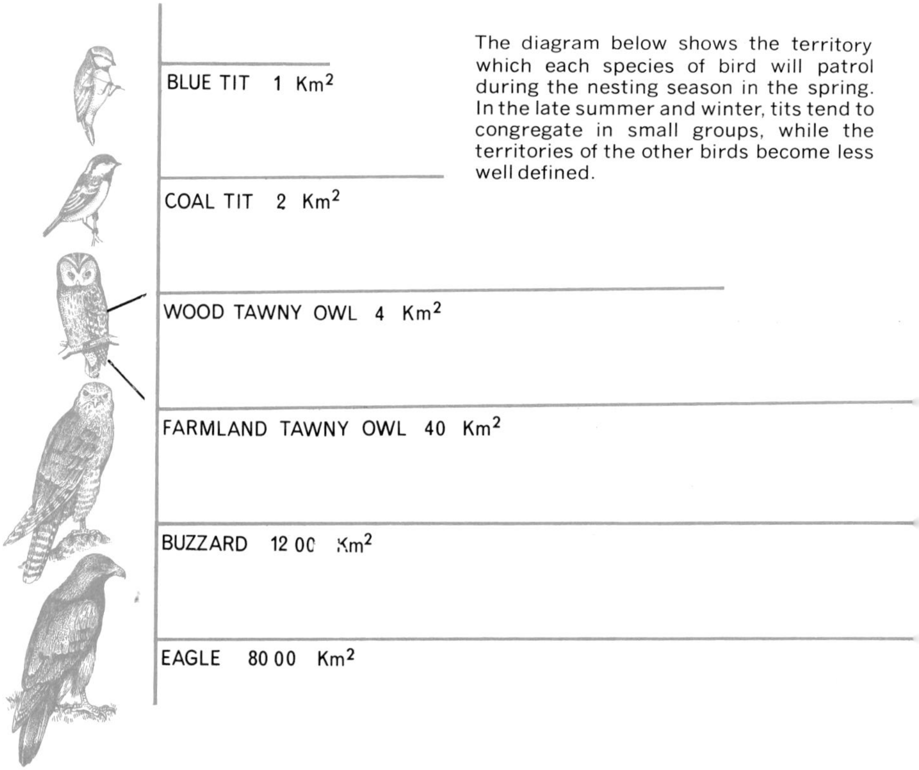

The diagram below shows the territory which each species of bird will patrol during the nesting season in the spring. In the late summer and winter, tits tend to congregate in small groups, while the territories of the other birds become less well defined.

BLUE TIT   1 Km²

COAL TIT   2 Km²

WOOD TAWNY OWL   4 Km²

FARMLAND TAWNY OWL   40 Km²

BUZZARD   12 00 Km²

EAGLE   80 00 Km²

Herons nest in colonies called heronries, building their untidy nests from large twigs. Outside the heronries they give up their social behaviour and spread out separately along the waterways and lakes to catch their food.

than if several pairs used the same lake. On the other hand, this behaviour means that every pond will have one pair of coots. It is possible that this arrangement is effective if, for instance, a lake completely dries up. Then at least only one pair of coots perishes, and others on other lakes will still flourish and produce their chicks. If many pairs of coots lived on one lake and there was some natural catastrophe, then large numbers would be lost.

On the other hand, there are a number of birds that go to the opposite extreme and nest together in large numbers. Herons in heronries and rooks in rookeries are obvious examples. But in these cases there are ways in which the birds live together that prevent the numbers of nests growing too great and make sure that the area of the colony is limited. If a bird builds in the 'wrong' place, then its nest will be taken apart, but it is most difficult to understand why herons should nest together in colonies. Possibly, because they nest together in trees which grow close together in woods, they protect each other, since as rather obvious light-coloured and large birds they are badly camouflaged. Since there are so many birds in a nesting colony they are protected by sheer number against hungry predators. But, if this is so, why do swans not also nest in colonies?

Cross-Section of a Pond

Ponds and shallow lakes can be particularly rich in life. Usually fringed by reeds, rushes and sedges, they also have a rich floating and underwater plant life. Animals may feed on these plants, lay eggs on them or crawl over them. Decaying plants are also eaten; if not, their remains will be broken down to provide nutrients which are reabsorbed to continue the food cycle. The diagram shows some of the inhabitants and the levels at which they are found.

1 Pond sponge, *Euspongilla lacustris*.
2 Green hydra, *Hydra viridis*.
3 Moss animalcule (Polyzoa), *Plumatella fruticosa*.
4 Flatworm, *Dugesia lugubris*.
5 Horse leech, *Haemopsis sanguisuga*.
6 Common water flea, *Daphnia pulex*.
7 Freshwater shrimp, *Gammarus*.
8 Water spider, *Argyroneta aquatica*.
9 Mayfly, *Ephemera vulgata*.

10 Water beetle, *Velia caprai.*
11 Water beetle, *Hydroporus pictus.*
12 Mosquito larva, *Culex.*
13 Great pond snail, *Limnaea stagnalis.*
14 Emperor dragonfly, *Anax imperator.*
15 Perch, *Perca fluviatilis.*
16 Pike, *Esox lucius.*
17 Bloodworm, *Tubifex.*
18 Spiked water milfoil, *Myriophyllum spicatum.*

19 Canadian pondweed, *Elodea canadensis.*
20 Pond lily, *Nymphae alba.*
21 Starwort, *Callitriche verna.*
22 Great duckweed, *Lemna polyrrhiza.*
23 Frogbit, *Hydrocharis morsus-ranae.*
24 Meadowsweet, *Filipendula ulmaria.*
25 Mud sedge, *Carex limosa.*
26 Purple loosestrife, *Lythrum salicaria.*

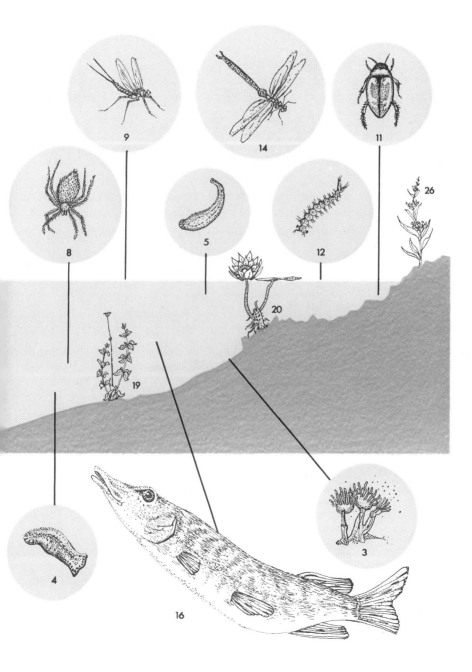

The Wood in Autumn

Hazelnuts, conkers, blackberries, elderberries, rose-hips and the early mountain-ash berries glowing in clusters bright as fluorescent beads. Old-man's-beard climbing in grey-white sheets over hawthorns and brambles along the edge of the wood. Beech leaves, chestnut leaves, oak leaves all colours, hanging still on a bright October afternoon, or pelting down-wind along the wet ground in a November storm. A high wind at Hallowe'en and all the leaves can be gone in a night, like a holiday crowd from a seaside town. I love to see the leafless shapes of the trees reappear—the beech trunks glistening in the rain and their upper twigs, perhaps, latticing a yellow, rainy sunset sky. A sound somewhere of water, the smell of sodden leaves and an old horse in the field outside staring over the fence into the wood and scratching himself on a wet gatepost as the redbreast sings. The redbreast twitters, really—little, sweet-toned phrases, as sharp and alert as himself. Almost always he sings to assert himself and lay claim to his own patch. If you watch him at it, you'll see that he sings a phrase or two and then stops and listens: and if you listen too, you can often hear another redbreast singing back at him from a little way off. They're laying claim, now the migrants have gone, to their winter feeding-grounds.

Autumn is a very good time to find toadstools and fungi, and such pleasure is to be got from these that it always surprises me that so many people either think they're nasty or else have never realized that they're worth looking at. In the first place, most of them can be eaten and a lot of them, like the wood mushroom, are in fact very good. Contrary to what a lot of people think, very few are poisonous. But be careful. One is the fly agaric (scarlet with white spots), though this would be unlikely actually to kill you. Another is the death cap, and this really is a dangerous killer, which you need to be able to recognize. Well, never mind about eating them: just to find and recognize them is delightful. I myself have a soft spot for bracket fungi—that is, fungi without stems, which grow as parasites on wood, living or dead, or on walls or stones. One of the prettiest is *Tramates versicolor* (it has no English name as far as I know), which can, as a matter of fact, be found at all times of the year. It often grows in tiered clusters, on dead wood or even among stones. The upper surface is beautifully marked, with alternating bands of colour which are astonishingly variable, depending on the place, the weather, the climate, the 'host' wood and so on. Red, chestnut, grey, ochre, green and blue are all quite common. I can remember finding a really startling, bright blue and green cluster, growing out of a dry-stone wall in Eskdale in Cumberland. Of other kinds of fungus, not brackets, a good one is the orange peel, which grows on the bare ground in autumn woods and looks (oddly enough) just like orange peel. Another is the witches' butter, which grows on dead oak branches. Other names are candle snuff, dead men's fingers, King Alfred's cakes, shaggy ink cap, spindly foot and dryad's saddle— quite a striking lot. It's well worth getting a book about toadstools and fungi. When you've got to know a few, you'll be astonished how various, delicate and beautiful they are.

Key to Illustration on pages 60-61

ANIMALS

1 Marsh tit 2 Nuthatch 3 Small copper 4 Small heath 5 Speckled wood 6 Common blue

PLANTS AND TREES

7 Wych 8 Ash 9 Oak 10 Maple 11 Beech 12 Sessile oak 13 Rowan 14 Birch 15 Elm 16 Sycamore 17 Small-leaved lime 18 Holly 19 Tree stump of elm 20 Tree stump of oak 21 Hazel 22 Hawthorn 23 Saint John's wort 24 Rose bay 25 Creeping cinquefoil 26 Ivy 27 Ivy flowers 28 Large wintergreen 29 Herb bennet 30 Bracken 31 Wood sorrel 32 Funnel cap 33 Death cap 34 Fly agaric 35 Wood sedge 36 Witches' butter 37 Earth star fungus

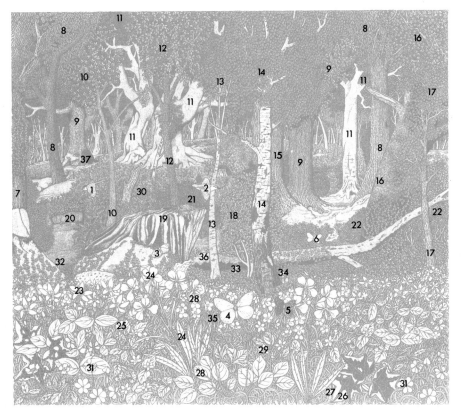

Fungi, Bacteria and the Cycling of Elements

Autumn is the time of the year to search for mushrooms in the meadows. You can also look for blewits and chanterelles in the woods. This is the time when the leaves of trees die, turn brown and fall. Fungi (which include moulds and slimes) grow on the decaying organic matter which the dead leaves provide. Most fungi live on dead matter, but some, such as the Dutch elm disease fungus, live on live wood. Fungi and bacteria do a very important job. Plants absorb carbon, nitrogen, potassium and phosphorus, four very important chemical substances. If fungi did not cause decay and break down the *compounds* which these chemical elements form, the stores of these substances in the world would be seriously lessened. They break down the chemical compounds, so that these *elements* can be used again by plants.

Plants provide food for fungi and bacteria, which in turn break down the food to more simple chemicals, which are in turn taken up by the plants. Thus there is a cycle or circular movement of chemicals. For instance, nitrogen, a gas which is found in the air, is also found in fallen leaves in the form of very complicated chemicals called proteins and amino acids (which have large groups of atoms called molecules). Bacteria, which are so small they can hardly be seen under an ordinary microscope, break down these substances into ammonia, and the ammonia is changed to nitrates. Once it has changed to nitrates it can be again taken up by the

The fungi illustrated here all have an important part to play in the recycling of vegetable matter. The bracket fungus (1) grows on conifers and attacks the wood itself; the slime fungus (2) grows on dead wood, and is here shown in its fruiting stage, about to produce spores in late summer and autumn. The sulphur tuft (3) grows all round the year on stumps, and the ear fungus (4) is particularly common on the bark of living elder.

roots of plants as food. In the meadow, of course, much of the possible nitrogen is not part of this cycle, because it has been taken away when the hay is cut, or has been eaten when animals graze on the grasses and other plants. So sometimes the farmer has to put nitrogen fertilizer into the soil to add the lost nitrogen and give the plants more to live off. But nature is very clever and there are some plants which have bacteria living *with* them which can actually capture free nitrogen and put it back into the soil. Some of the bacteria live by themselves, but others live in bubble-like structures on the roots of plants in the pea family, such as clovers. Farmers often encourage clover to grow with the grass, or they plant a crop of plants in the pea family to put nitrogen back into the soil.

Not all nitrogen in the soil gets there from pea family plants or from fertilization. Rain can wash nitrogen compounds from the leaves of plants. Only one fifth of the nitrogen is put back into the soil in this way, but since the rain also carries one third of the phosphate requirements and two thirds of the potassium requirements back into the soil this is a very important part of the nourishment of the soil. Small amounts of sugars are also washed down in the rain, but sugars are usually used first by fungi, and unlike the potassium and the phosphorus compounds are not directly absorbed by plants. Sugar, like starch, cellulose, lignin (which partly forms the woodiness of trees) and other substances, is based on carbon. The breakdown of the carbon compounds is largely dependent on fungi. Each of these carbon compounds is attacked by different groups of fungi which arrive on the decaying plant in succession. First to arrive are the fungi which break down sugar and starch. These fungi are moulds such as you might find on a piece of stale bread. A little later, other fungi set to work and these can break down the cellulose compounds. So when you see a piece of wood or a leaf rotting, you must remember that several different fungi are working to break it down into fairly simple chemical compounds that can then be absorbed by plants and built up into their complicated stems, leaves, flowers, roots, etc. In the meadow, where cellulose is commoner than lignin, you may only see fairy ring toadstools and ordinary mushrooms. These are among the larger fungi which work on breaking down cellulose.

In woods there is a much greater variety of larger fungi, many of which specialize in destroying lignin. You may well see one of these, such as the beefsteak fungus, on the branch of an oak.

The blewit (5) and the chanterelle (6) are both edible. They grow in the rich soil of deciduous woodlands.

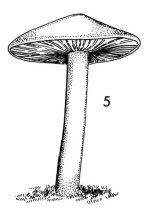

Mushrooms and Toadstools

In fields and woods, especially in the autumn, you will see some of the fungi in these pages. Some are poisonous, and they are shown opposite (marked with a red dot beside the illustration). But many are very good to eat. Always make absolutely certain that you know the most poisonous fungi, and never eat anything unless you are sure it is safe; and always cook fungi well.

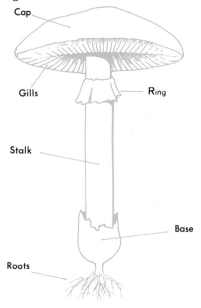

Cap

Gills

Ring

Stalk

Base

Roots

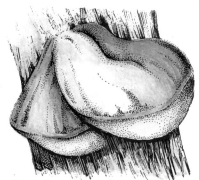

Beefsteak fungus, *Fistulina hepatica*. Oak tree trunks. August-October. Eat when young.

Common puff-ball, *Lycoperdon perlatum*. Grassy places. June-November. Eat when flesh is white.

If you place the cap of a mushroom, gills down, on a piece of white paper, after a while you will have a spore print. This can be done with many fungi. See how many colours of spores there are.

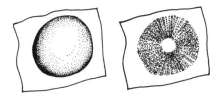

On a lawn or on closely grazed turf you may find there is sometimes a ring of small fungi or a ring of darker green grass. This is often caused by the fairy ring champignon *(Marasmius oreades)*. Every year the ring spreads by 15-30 cm. There are some huge 'fairy rings' which are centuries old.

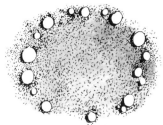

Parasol mushroom, *Lepiota procera*. Clearings or edge of wood. July-October. Delicious, but stems tough.

Field (or button) mushroom, *Agaricus campestris*. Grassy places. May-November. This is the mushroom sold in shops.

There are not many very poisonous fungi, but some will cause acute indigestion. The most important one to recognize, as it can kill you, is the death cap *(Amanita phalloides)*. The cap is yellowish-green (occasionally pale brown or white) and the gills and spores are *white*. It rarely grows in fields or meadows.

Fairy cake (or poison pie), *Hebeloma crustuliniforme.* Woods and gardens. August-November. Poisonous.

Fly agaric, *Amanita muscaria.* Under birch or pine trees. August-November. Poisonous.

Common ink cap, *Coprinus atramentarius.* Gardens and along ditches. June-November. Slightly poisonous.

Verdigris agaric, *Stropharia aeruginosa.* Pasture and grassy places in woods. July-November. Poisonous.

Death cap, *Amanita phalloides.* Mainly woods. July-October. DEADLY. Beware, when young, this can look very like both the common puff-ball and the field mushroom.

The sickener, *Russula emetica.* Woods. July-November. Slightly poisonous.

The Lake and Stream in Autumn

In the changeable weather of autumn, a river and its banks—always a place of variety and movement—seem to assume different moods day by day—sometimes almost hour by hour. On a warm, sunny October afternoon, under the thinning, red and yellow-leaved branches of the horse chestnuts spreading over the water, the chub bubble the surface of the brown pools, rising to take the big, torpid sedge flies or sometimes an unlucky grasshopper or wasp that has fallen in and is drifting down the current. Chub are no good to eat, but on such a golden, still day to fish for them with a dry fly can be good sport, and gives a last taste of summer, gentle and melancholy as the cooler sun begins its early setting. Many of the wild flowers are still in bloom on the banks; the old indestructibles—ragwort, shepherd's purse, purple knapweed, blue tufts of selfheal, and herb robert with its geranium-scented leaves.

I remember one unusually warm October afternoon, many years ago, an old friend dared me and we went swimming in a weir-pool in the river Kennet below Newbury. The swallows had been gone a good fortnight. The leaves were falling into the white water and drifting downstream all around us, and a thrush was shouting from the top of an ash tree. It is the only time that I have ever gone swimming in a river in October; and it was well worth doing. In a country where weather is as unpredictable as in England, one should always be on one's toes to seize happy and unexpected opportunities; not only for themselves, but because they make such fine memories.

Next day the wind may be up, and all the autumnal tranquility will be blown out of a sky of racing clouds and a stream that wrinkles and slides under the sharp gusts. The aspen and poplar leaves come flying down in yellow showers, pelting and twirling until they strike the water; and then stop as sharply as a moth flying into a sheet of glass. At such times, one can hear the altered sound of the fuller river, swollen by rain—the slower, deeper rippling and the heavy pouring of the weirs, their sluices opened to take the increased flow. There may already have been some frost at night, and the sedges are withered, rasping in the wind with a sound very different from the rustling of summer. But if it is still early autumn—late September or early October—another, happier sound may be the dying fall of the willow warbler's song. He is the last warbler to leave, and sometimes stays into a fine October, well after the swallows have gone.

In late autumn, under a darkened, silver-gleaming sunset or stormy nightfall, the river will be sombre, mysterious, even a little forbidding. Mist rises into the chilly air, curling among the bare, trailing willows. The silent flow of the river itself seems part of the stillness, unbroken except, perhaps, for the sudden alighting of a pair of mallards; the passing of two or three swans, continually thrusting and withdrawing their long necks as they forage on the bottom; or the harsh, vibrant cry

74

of an unseen moorhen echoing across the water. At such times it is easy to realize that the water has flowed uninterrupted for centuries. In this falling, autumnal twilight you cannot tell, from the river, what century it is. Perhaps it was under such a nightfall that Housman remembered the river of his home country.

Far in a western brookland
That bred me long ago
The poplars stand and tremble
By pools I used to know.

There, by the starlit fences,
The wanderer halts and hears
My soul that lingers sighing
About the glimmering weirs.

Key to Illustration on pages 76-77

ANIMALS

1 Mute swan 2 Bearded tit 3 Mallard 4 Teal 5 Pochard 6 Pintail 7 Shoveler (female) 8 Tufted duck 9 Moorhen

PLANTS AND TREES

10 Willow (pollarded) 11 Alders 12 Oak 13 Reeds 14 Reedmace (bulrush) 15 Touch-me-not 16 Common watercress 17 Brooklime 18 Soapwort 19 Common water dropwort 20 Creeping yellow cress 21 Common chickweed 22 Coot's nest 23 Reed sweet-grass 24 Annual meadow-grass 25 Common spike-rush

Food Chain and Food Web

Plants and animals need food to give them energy. They also need food to provide material for growing. They can use carbon and nitrogen from the air, and phosphorus and potassium and sulphur from the earth. These elements all have their special part to play in the animal and plant lives. In ponds and streams, sulphur is often the most obvious chemical. When a fish such as a pike dies, sulphur which has been locked up in the proteins and amino acids of its body will be released into the water. Sulphur compounds often smell very unpleasant, like 'stink bombs', and this is why a dead animal can make such a nasty stench. When the fish dies, bacteria convert some of its body into sulphur compounds, like hydrogen sulphide, which can become trapped in the black mud at the bottom of the pond and give off a foul smell when stirred. But if the water is moving, as in a stream, and oxygen can reach the bottom, then other bacteria can exist, and they convert the foul-smelling 'bad egg' hydrogen sulphide into soluble sulphates which water plants can absorb and take up into their bodies. Then a fish—perhaps a carp—comes along and eats up the plant, and the sulphur that was once in the fish's body, and was then broken down to hydrogen sulphide and sulphates after the fish died, is taken up by the carp, who then might be eaten by a pike who eventually dies and the whole cycle is repeated.

This movement of energy and substances from one creature to another through eating (or absorbing) and being eaten is called *a food chain*. All food chains really start with green plants, which can capture energy from sunlight and by means of the green chlorophyll in their tissues can convert the sunlight to sugars and oxygen. All other animals— insects, birds, fish, mammals—depend on the presence of green plants. In water, the most important of these green plants can often be the least

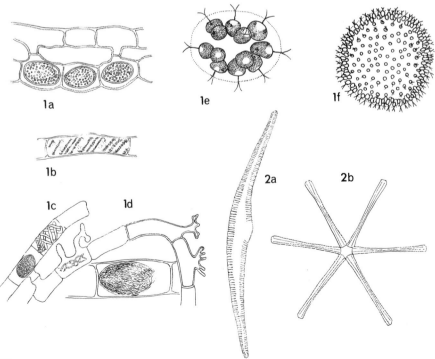

1a

1e

1f

1b

2a   2b

1c   1d

obvious—the very tiny plants called algae. When conditions are good for them, these algae can be seen as a green scum floating on the water. These conditions usually occur when there is extra nitrogen and phosphorus added to the water from sewage outfalls or from fertilizers being washed off the fields. But sometimes they occur in autumn in the deeper lakes when the surface of the water begins to cool. Though the surface water has had all its food substances used up during the summer, as it cools it sinks and so the whole lake becomes mixed up, and sulphur, for instance, in the deeper parts, gets brought up to the surface again so that it provides a good food base for the algae. These deep-water foods were not used up during the summer, partly because of the colder temperatures lower down and partly because there was not enough sunlight deep down to give the algae energy to grow and feed.

This all means that life is richer in shallow waters or in waters, such as streams, where water is continually being mixed. But the flow of water in a running stream or river is a mixed blessing, since unless the algae are attached to stones or rooted plants they are washed away. Where fast streams do have algae and mosses attached to stones, they can be quite full of life, for hidden in the tufts of moss, and perhaps feeding on them, are minute animals, and snails will slide over the stones eating the algae coating them.

A slower stream, with wider pools, will have many more plants rooted in the mud at its edges, and here, in the still water, you can find dragonfly nymphs, the burrowing nymphs of mayflies and caddis fly larvae, with their curious cases made of sticks, leaves, stones, grains of sand or pieces of shell.

Caddis fly larvae are part of a food chain which leads to us, for they eat plants, and they themselves are eaten by trout which we, when we can catch them, eat at our tables.

Algae are simple plants which range from the scum on ponds to 30-metre-long seaweeds. Their variety is enormous, but they can easily be differentiated from some other simple plants, such as fungi, because they contain chlorophyll. A few examples of freshwater algae from various groups are shown here; some are visible to the naked eye (e.g. Spirogyra, Volvox). In some conditions, such as pollution by agricultural fertilizers, numbers of algae increase alarmingly and can choke waterways, a process called 'eutrophication'. But in normal circumstances they are an important part of the food chain and are browsed on by animals as large as fish.

1 GREEN ALGAE: (a) Spirogyra aequi-noctialis, (b) Cell showing chloroplasts and numerous pyrenoids, (c) Spirogyra rhizo-brachiales, (d) Zygospore, (e) Volvox tertius, (f) Pandorina morum.

2 DIATOMS: (a) Ceratoneis arcus, (b) Asterionella formosa.

3 BLUE-GREEN ALGAE: (a) Calothrix epiphytica, (b) Calothrix atricha, (c) Calothrix Braunii.

4 DESMIDS: (a) Micrasterias americanum, (b) Micrasterias radiata, (c) Micrasterias foliacea.

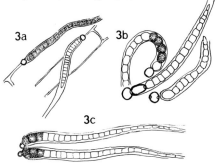

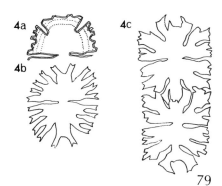

Plant Life in Various Altitudes and Latitudes

Temperature and rainfall are amongst the most important aspects of climate, and it is the changes in these going up a mountain, or travelling north, which produce the strikingly similar sequence of natural communities.

As air is forced to rise over a mountain range it cools and any moisture it contains condenses out as clouds and eventually as rain. A rise in altitude of 300 metres is roughly equivalent to moving 250 kilometres farther north.

Although the altitude diagram is based on the Sierra Nevada in California, the same zones can be seen on any other mountain range. There will, however, usually be fewer of them because either the mountains are not as high, or they are farther north.

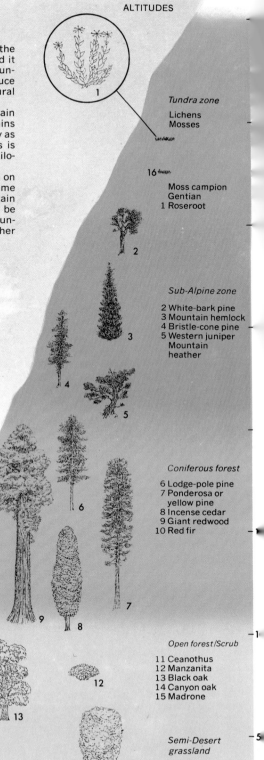

ALTITUDES

Tundra zone

Lichens
Mosses

Moss campion
Gentian
1 Roseroot

Sub-Alpine zone

2 White-bark pine
3 Mountain hemlock
4 Bristle-cone pine
5 Western juniper
Mountain
heather

Coniferous forest

6 Lodge-pole pine
7 Ponderosa or
yellow pine
8 Incense cedar
9 Giant redwood
10 Red fir

Open forest/Scrub

11 Ceanothus
12 Manzanita
13 Black oak
14 Canyon oak
15 Madrone

Semi-Desert grassland

Brome
Blue grass
Wild rye

80

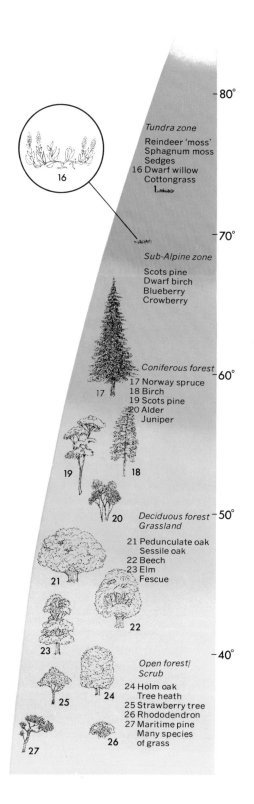

PERMANENT SNOW. Little can live in this zone apart from a few simple organisms.

TUNDRA/ALPINE ZONE. Rainfall is low, but, because of the permafrost (continuously frozen ground), it cannot drain away and so the ground in summer is permanently waterlogged. Myriads of mosquitoes and similar insects breed here and attract large numbers of migrant birds to breed.
Plants tend to be low-growing perennials which flower quickly after the snow melts so that the seed can ripen in the short summer.

SUB-ALPINE ZONE. A narrow zone of scattered and stunted trees between the tundra and the forest proper. This zone is much better represented on the mountains and is the zone in which the flower-covered mountain meadows occur, *the alps*, after which the European mountain range is named.

NORTHERN CONIFEROUS FOREST ZONE. Some of the world's largest trees belong to this zone, for example the giant redwoods *(Sequoiadendron giganteum)* of the Sierras.
The trees are almost all evergreen with needle-like leaves so that they can make maximum use of the short growing season but at the same time shed the winter snows before the branches break.

DECIDUOUS FOREST/STEPPES ZONE. This zone is not represented in the Sierras, but is present on other mountains.
The forests occur in the temperate zone where wet winds blow onshore. As the winds lose their rain, there is eventually too little to support trees and they are replaced by the broad grasslands of central Eurasia and North America.

OPEN WOODLAND SCRUB/ZONE. This community is composed of bushes with leathery leaves, which produce masses of flowers in the spring after the winter rains. They quickly fall dormant again, however, with the onset of the long, hot, dry summer. This type of community is familiar to all who live in the American south-west or have visited southern Europe. It has many names, e.g. maquis, chaparral, mattoral.

SEMI-DESERT GRASSLAND ZONE. The narrow belt at the edge of the desert proper where the rainfall is too irregular even for the scrub. The grass survives by having a large spreading root system to absorb as much of the infrequent rain as possible. Many desert 'annuals' are also found here. They grow and flower in a matter of a week or two after rain, leaving their seeds dormant in the soil until the next storm.

Tundra zone

Reindeer 'moss'
Sphagnum moss
Sedges
16 Dwarf willow
Cottongrass
1

Sub-Alpine zone

Scots pine
Dwarf birch
Blueberry
Crowberry

Coniferous forest
17 Norway spruce
18 Birch
19 Scots pine
20 Alder
Juniper

Deciduous forest
Grassland

21 Pedunculate oak
Sessile oak
22 Beech
23 Elm
Fescue

Open forest/
Scrub

24 Holm oak
Tree heath
25 Strawberry tree
26 Rhododendron
27 Maritime pine
Many species
of grass

80°

70°

60°

50°

40°

The Wood in Winter

The holly bears a prickle, as sharp as any thorn;
And Mary bore sweet Jesus Christ on Christmas day in the morn.

The holly still makes a brave show and everyone likes to see it, particularly at Christmas. But in the world of today, where bright colours are regarded as a matter of course, it has lost most, though not all, of the almost magical effect it used to have in years gone by. Even as recently as a hundred and fifty years ago, most country people saw very little brilliant colour and in winter there was almost none. In those days, the sight of the holly in December—the crisp, close-set, curling leaves shining glossy in the sun, and the sprays of scarlet berries—must have caught people's attention far more vividly than ever they can today. The children of yesteryear, who knew nothing of sugar and little of honey, were ready to risk a beating to steal apples. They craved for something sweet, and in the same way—through deprivation—they craved for colour too. To simple, ignorant people, the holly was clearly magical—the prickles sharp as thorns, the berries red as blood, the evergreen leaves staunch against frost, storm and snow. It was plainly a symbol of Christ, and must have been created for that purpose. Superstition, of course—but we still don't care to be without evergreens at Christmas; holly, ivy, and sometimes bay and ilex too. The holly is common throughout Britain and you can find one in most woods, and often along the hedgerows too.

When I think of woods in winter, what I chiefly call to mind is silence; and the wind. On a still day, especially if it is frosty, a wood is often almost disturbingly silent. The sound of a stick snapping underfoot is enough to set the wood pigeons clattering away among the bare oak branches. No leaves to rustle, no insects to buzz, no bird-song. But at other times, in rough weather, the wind penetrates the woods as it never can in summer. Fear of the winter wind is another thing that we feel less deeply today than did people of long ago. Their clothes were often thin or ragged and many were obliged to be out of doors in winter whether they liked it or not; digging, getting in wood or tending beasts in the cold wind. Shakespeare mentions it again and again.

When all about the wind doth blow
And coughing drowns the parson's saw, [that means, his preaching]
And birds sit brooding in the snow
And Marian's nose looks red and raw—

And in *King Lear,* the line which to me remains the keynote of the whole play is Edgar's 'Still through the hawthorn blows the cold wind'. In those days the woods were deeper and thicker than they are now, and the moaning of the wind through the bare trees must have kept people continually in mind of the forlorn wildness, even when they were indoors. We often say we enjoy the winter, but what we really mean is that we enjoy feeling proof against it. For wild animals and birds it remains hard—desperate, sometimes, for food is scarce and without food one soon dies of the cold if one can't get out of it. This is, in fact, how most birds die.

The world is very old, and I never feel more aware of this than in a wood in winter—partly, I think, because of solitude, and the early-falling darkness of the short afternoon: and because of the dead leaves underfoot, the great, empty trees that no longer shut out the grey sky—and the wind. How bleak the rooks' nests look, tossing against a grey sky as the light fails! This planet we live on is hospitable only in certain places and at certain times of year. It is good for us to be reminded of that, sometimes; to scatter some bread in the wood (even if the rats get most of it), come home out of the cold and be glad of a fire.

Key to Illustration on pages 84-85

ANIMALS

1 Red deer 2 Rook 3 Hooded crow

PLANTS AND TREES

4 Wych elm 5 Ash 6 Oak 7 Maple 8 Beech 9 Sessile oak 10 Rowan 11 Birch 12 Elm
13 Sycamore 14 Small-leaved lime 15 Tree stump of elm 16 Tree stump of oak 17 Holly
18 Hawthorn 19 Hazel 20 Ivy 21 Barren strawberry 22 Primrose 23 Winter aconite
24 Snowdrop 25 Stinking hellebore 26 Razor strop 27 Chanterelle 28 Elf cup
29 Bracken 30 Wood meadow-grass 31 Wood melick 32 Wood false brome grass
33 Earth star fungus

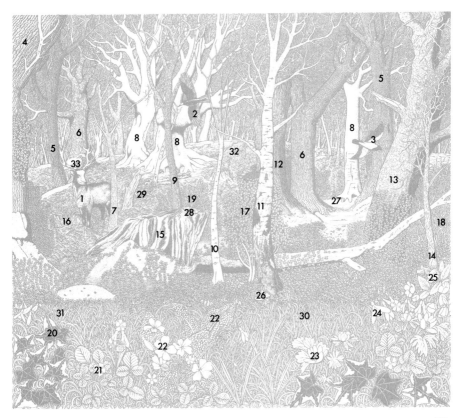

Overwintering and Hibernation

As winter approaches, the days become shorter and the weather is usually colder and damper. Food supplies get scarcer and some animals and plants have a hard time keeping alive. But many animals and plants have managed to avoid the cold or food shortages by a variety of means. Some, like the swallow and the cuckoo, migrate to sunnier places, such as Africa. Others go into a state of *diapause* or *dormancy*. Both diapause (in insects) and dormancy (in buds and seeds) are rather like sleep, but the insects and plants stop developing until they are switched on again at the end of the diapause or dormancy. More advanced animals sometimes overcome bad conditions by going into a state of sleep called *hibernation* or winter sleep. (In very hot, dry climates, animals may avoid the high temperatures and drought by going into a similar state of sleep—this time called *aestivation* or summer sleep.)

There are different 'switches' which turn the diapause, dormancy or hibernation on and off, but the commonest are connected with temperature and the length of daylight. There is a striped yellow-and-black beetle called the Colorado beetle. You may never see one, since it is a terrible pest of the potato crops and everything has been done to wipe it out entirely. But because it is such a pest, it has been carefully studied by scientists and we know quite a lot about it. The adult lays eggs from May to April. When the orange-yellow grub (or larva) is hatched, it will then shed its skin (moult) three times before burrowing into the soil to pupate. After a fortnight, the adult beetle emerges and is active from July to September. In a good summer some of these adults may lay eggs, but in a bad summer (and in most cases in a good summer too) they will gorge themselves with as much food as they can obtain for two weeks and then burrow back into the soil (even as early as August) and enter the sleeping state we call diapause.

What makes them burrow? It has been found that there is a special length of day which triggers off the burrowing instinct. If there are less than fifteen hours of light, the beetles start their greedy fortnight's feeding and then burrow. If there are more than fifteen hours of light, they will continue to feed as long as food is available. If the food becomes scarce they burrow and go into diapause. We do not know exactly what wakes

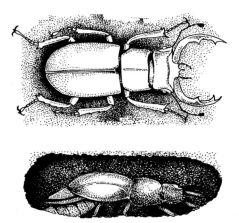

The Colorado beetle feeds greedily on potato leaves before hibernating in winter. The stag beetle burrows beneath the ground to spend the cold winter days.

In the horse chestnut the buds ('sticky buds') lie dormant over winter, though, as the diagram shows, all the leaves and flower parts are ready to unfurl in spring.

them from diapause. Most insects emerge after being chilled by the passing winter, but Colorado beetles sleep longer if they are chilled.

In plants, similar behaviour is called dormancy, and the buds of trees are very often dormant in winter. As long as the days are long, they produce leaves, but with the shorter days they form dormant buds. Not all trees do this. Apples, pears and plums, the ash and the lilac, all seem insensitive to the length of day. But generally speaking, woody plants form dormant buds, and their dormancy is broken by the chill of winter. You can 'wake' buds from dormancy by keeping them in a refrigerator, but this must be done for at least two weeks and with some plants for as long as two months.

Some plants, like the birch and the beech, will not respond to chilling. Others that are dormant underground, such as the sunflower, gladiolus and lily-of-the-valley, have their dormancy broken by chilling. Yet the potato actually sprouts more rapidly when the temperature rises.

The mammals which hibernate are mostly insect-eaters. Bats can be seen hanging upside down in dark places from October to April. They are unusual in that they mate before hibernation, but the baby bats do not start to grow inside them until hibernation is over. Hedgehogs and rodents, on the other hand, follow the more common pattern of mating after hibernation and producing their offspring before returning to hibernate the following October.

Mammals live at a lower temperature than normal when hibernating. Bats can even be kept in a refrigerator, but their temperature control is so efficient that they have warmed themselves up enough to fly within fifteen minutes of being taken out of the cold. Their temperature switch has been turned up, enabling them to burn their stored food more quickly and so warm themselves up. On mild winter days animals may wake up from hibernation and forage for food. The dormouse, which seems to sleep deepest of all, will even lay up stocks of food near its nest, in case it wakes up by mistake.

87

Animal Hibernation

Squirrels, both the red and North American grey species, spend the harsher winter days and nights hibernating. After they have collected their autumn fruits— mainly nuts, which they bury in the ground —they hibernate in their 'dreys', nests made of twigs. When spring comes they 'wake up' again and can be seen digging for their buried hoards of food.

The uncommon smooth snake, which is of course cold-blooded and must therefore avoid the possibility of freezing solid in a bad winter, simply curls up tightly in a dry, sheltered place beneath the thick heather which covers the sandy heaths where it lives. On warm days in early spring it will make exploratory, though rather sluggish, outings in search of its prey.

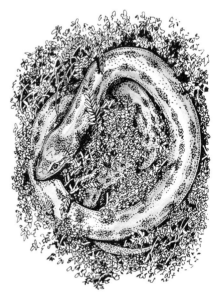

The attractive Painted Lady is a migrant butterfly which comes from the Mediterranean and usually returns there in the autumn. However, some stay to hibernate and like other members of the family may be found sleeping on rafters in dark places or in hollow trees. Peacocks and Small Tortoiseshells are much easier to find than the rather uncommon Painted Lady.

The very common pipistrelle bat hibernates in sheltered dark places such as barns, attics, high up in churches and in hollow trees. It spends its winter hanging upside down and often forms part of a large group which clusters together for warmth and so saves some of the energy which would otherwise be spent fending off the cold. Hibernation lasts from October until April.

Ladybirds can sometimes be found hibernating in groups of many individuals. The places to look for them are under loose tree bark or in the corners of window frames and other similar places indoors.

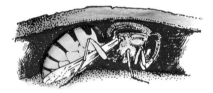

Hedgehogs can sometimes be heard snoring, while they hibernate at the bottom of a hedgerow or in some equally protected place. They cover themselves with leaves, grass and moss and are thus hard to spot. They usually spend October to March in hibernation, but if the weather is warm they frequently come out to forage for food.

The queen tree wasp hibernates under the bark of a tree. Tree wasps, like the common wasp, are social insects living in colonies, but the males die after mating and the queen is left to form the new colony in the spring.

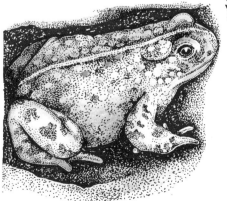

Natterjack toads will find a dark hole, usually below ground level and often under a stone, where they spend the winter almost completely inert. Indeed, if you are lucky enough to discover one hibernating, it will look dead. Common toads will sometimes congregate together in a deep pit or dry well where there is a covering of leaves.

The Meadow and Hedgerow in Winter

Both in the green, mild weather which we generally get during the earlier part of winter—November and December—and in the harder weather which often follows Christmas, one can often walk all day through lanes, fields, heather and downland without seeing much out of the ordinary, or anything to get excited about. Of course, you never know your luck. You may happen upon a hungry fox on his way to raid some cottage dustbins, or see a kestrel drop on a mouse made slow by the cold. I once found a very lively woolly bear caterpillar in the grass near the White Horse of Uffington on Boxing Day. A hare, lolloping like a low-flying rocking-chair, may come towards you down a lane, approach to within fifteen feet as you stand still, watching; and then suddenly get your wind and dash away down the hedge. Or a cock-pheasant may get up from under your feet in a flash of red, green and chestnut, exploding like an alarm-rocket. But more often there will be quietness and a certain emptiness, broken by nothing more exciting than the steaming breath of cows round a gate, or a flock of sparrows or hen-chaffinches tussling their way down a bare hedge where the dusk-red, worm-channelled leaves still cling to the bramble-sprays.

For this reason some people feel that it is better, if you are going out at this time of year, to go out for sport—riding, shooting, or fishing for pike, perhaps; or skating, if the ice is bearing. But walking can be enjoyable too, especially on hills and if there is no winter fog or mist to obscure the bare, open country. There is a clean emptiness about the polished furrows of the ploughed fields and the high, cold sky—and no gnats to bite you if you feel warm enough to sit down to enjoy the view. In some of the fields there may be flood-patches of bright, shallow water, where flocks of gulls are paddling and stabbing about.. Most of these will be black-headed gulls (but not black-headed all the year round—they moult in summer and black up again in late winter: the black head is 'mating dress'), but with luck there may also be some of the bigger herring gulls; and even terns and oyster-catchers, if the weather has been stormy and you are not too far from the sea.

If the winter sunset is fine (yellow and silver; or perhaps a frosty one—ice-green and cinder-red) the rooks will be playing their beautiful gliding, sailing games in the sky. Round and round they go, rising and falling, sometimes hardly moving a wing for minutes together, playing with the air currents. Stand and watch them, and it is impossible to see what motive they can have but their own enjoyment. 'So nature pricken hem in hir corages', as Chaucer says of the birds. It could hardly be expressed more precisely.

Just as a true musician finds pleasure in very quiet-toned music as well as in colourfully-orchestrated, exciting stuff; or a true artist in a fine pencil-drawing as well as in a big, brightly-coloured painting; so a real nature-lover and countryman derives delight from the small things of winter in the fields—scarlet rose-hips and Robin's pincushions on the

90

briar; sprays of oakapples; the flat, wet clots of oak leaves sticking together like brown pancakes; the crunching of frosty long grass under gumboots; or the foxy, red-brown glow of bare willow branches in the late afternoon sun. And the stars come out early, and are already glittering in the frosty sky as one goes home to tea.

Key to Illustration on pages 92-93

ANIMALS

1 Stock dove 2 Jackdaw

PLANTS AND TREES

3 Oak 4 Maple 5 Ash 6 Elm 7 Sycamore trees 8 Beech 9 Hazel 10 Bramble
11 Blackthorn 12 Privet hedge 13 Hawthorn 14 Bracket fungus 15 Ivy 16 Primrose
17 Persian speedwell 18 Chickweed 19 Snowdrop 20 Winter aconite 21 Shepherd's purse
22 Dog rose 23 Coltsfoot 24 Annual meadow-grass 25 Meadow fescue-grass
26 Common rye-grass 27 Rough meadow-grass

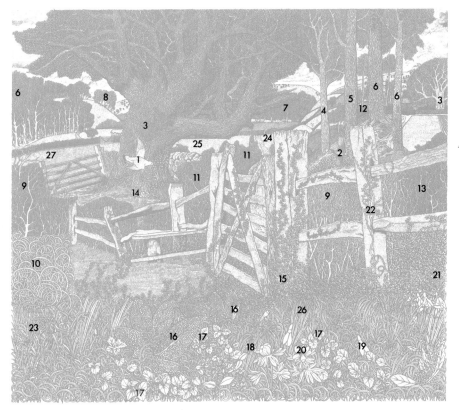

Animal Camouflage

The word camouflage is said to have come from the French word for a puff of smoke or smokescreen, so really we should only use it to describe cases where animals escape from an enemy by putting up some sort of smokescreen, perhaps like an octopus squirting its ink at an incautious aqualung diver or a bombadier beetle squirting its liquid when handled.

Of course we now use the word for a wide variety of cases where an enemy is avoided or at least put off by colours, definite patterns of colours, even shapes, or some combination of all three. Various animals have tried different techniques to make themselves invisible. About the most common method is to adopt some mottled pattern of colours so as to merge with the background as the nightjar does in woodland, mimicking a pattern of jumbled twigs with its speckled grey-brown feathers. Many moths look just like bits of twig or bark—the waved umber and peppered moth use this technique, while the festoon and lappet moths resemble dead leaves. During the last hundred years soot from factory chimneys near our big cities has been deposited on the bark of trees, and moths which rest during the day on a tree trunk have had to become darker if they live near towns to avoid being picked off and eaten by birds. Populations of peppered moth, grey arches, pale brindled beauty and poplar lutestring have become much darker near towns, while country cousins away from the smoke and grime remain light coloured. This change in their surroundings has taken many years and the moths have changed over generations, but sometimes an environment undergoes dramatic changes within one animal's lifetime. Where such changes are regular and predictable animals have adapted to being able to change their camouflage too. The most dramatic of these is perhaps the change from brown to white in some animals like the blue hare, stoat or ptarmigan which live where snow falls each winter. How white the stoat becomes in Britain is somewhat variable and may depend on temperature. The further north and hence more persistent the snows, the whiter the animals may have to be, until we have examples like the arctic fox which is grey above and white below in summer and all white in winter, and the polar bear which is white all the year round.

The nightjar (whip-poor-will) is a smallish brown bird, whose mottled feathers blend perfectly with the surroundings on the ground. A night-flier, it is best discovered by its very characteristic churring song.

94

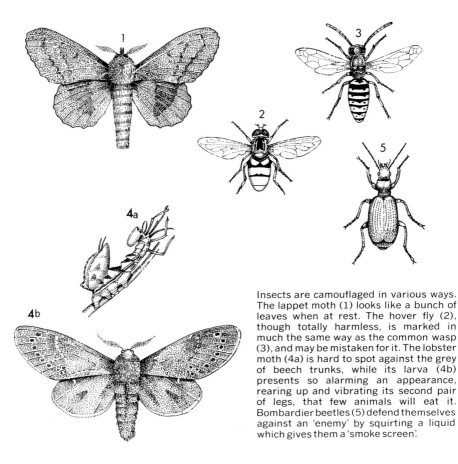

Insects are camouflaged in various ways. The lappet moth (1) looks like a bunch of leaves when at rest. The hover fly (2), though totally harmless, is marked in much the same way as the common wasp (3), and may be mistaken for it. The lobster moth (4a) is hard to spot against the grey of beech trunks, while its larva (4b) presents so alarming an appearance, rearing up and vibrating its second pair of legs, that few animals will eat it. Bombardier beetles (5) defend themselves against an 'enemy' by squirting a liquid which gives them a 'smoke screen'.

Yet more dramatic are those animals which can change colour almost at will like the chameleon. This, though the most famous, is not the only example. Flat fish on the bottom of the sea like the sole can do it, as can newts and frogs to a limited degree. There is even a spider—the crab spider—which can change from white to yellow and back again, albeit taking several days in the process. This spider lies in wait in flowers for unsuspecting pollinating insects like bees and can take on the colour of the flower, so that it isn't seen either by its own prey or by those that might prey on it.

Another sort of camouflage, usually known as *mimicry*, is where an animal takes on not only the colour but also the general shape of another which is either distasteful to the predator or too dangerous to attack. Thus hover flies (Syrphids) commonly look just like bees and wasps and presumably predators avoid them for fear of being stung, though in fact the hover flies have no sting.

The caterpillars of some moths too have evolved special shapes, as for example the Prominent which looks like the shape of the leaf margin which it eats. The caterpillars of the Blotched emerald actually decorate themselves with real bits of leaf as a disguise.

The most remarkable camouflage exhibited by any moth caterpillar is that of the lobster moth which if disturbed raises and bends back its front and waves its second pair of legs almost like a large ant, but it too can put up a smokescreen, for it has a gland which can eject formic acid—a poison—in sufficient quantity to put off any bird that might attack it.

95

Badgers have powerful claws with which they can excavate their deep burrows or 'sets', which are usually found in deciduous woods with a fair amount of undergrowth.

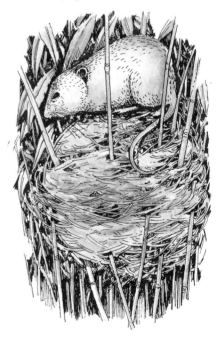

The harvest mouse constructs a nest of leaves and stalks woven into a hollow ball round the upright stalks of corn.

The otter often burrows beneath the roots of a waterside tree to create its 'holt'. This can sometimes be identified by the remains of frogs and fish which litter the entrance.

96

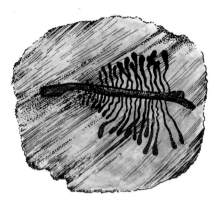

The larva of the spruce bark beetle constructs galleries in the roots and stumps of spruce. The main gallery may run for 5 cm.

Caddis-fly larvae cover their bodies with pieces of stone, sand, stick, shells, etc. Different species can be distinguished by the type of material they use to protect their soft bodies.

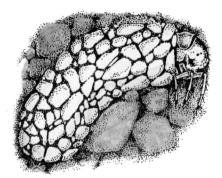

Leaf miners are larvae which feed on leaves, producing a winding passage through the middle layers which can easily be seen when held to the light. The caterpillar of the moth *Lyonetia clerckelle* feeds on birch leaves and leaves a dark trail of excreta down its winding 'mine'.

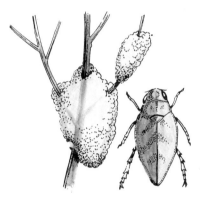

The tiny nymphs of the froghopper produce a frothy liquid, the well-known cuckoo-spit, in which they live, feeding on the juice of the plant they have settled on, until they are fully grown.

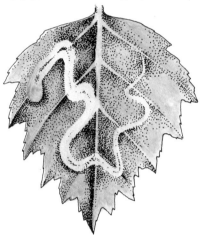

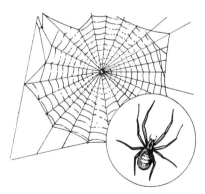

The common black ant constructs a simple system of galleries or narrow tunnels, excavated in the earth beneath stones, logs or under the walls of a building. These nests are built by the worker ants.

Garden spiders produce the well-known and beautiful webs. These are incredibly strong for the thickness of the silk. The spider rests in the centre of the web and any insect caught produces vibrations, which rouse the spider who hurries off to consume its prey.

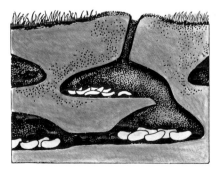

The Lake and Stream in Winter

Is there any place that seems so remote and still as a lake in winter? The very sound of the word 'mere' suggests the expanse of dully shining, motionless water, the grey reed-beds and bare woods behind; and perhaps, far off, from one end of the lake, enclosed in trees, the pouring of the outfall over its rocky cascade. Along the shore, here and there, rise tall heads of reedmace six or seven feet high—green last June, but now withered to furry-brown, velvety bell-sallies. Big pike may be lying torpid among the watery shallows, their tails faintly moving, their sides speckled with pale lemon spots like snowflakes. Unlike the trout, there is no tempting them when they are not hungry—no bait will excite them out of their lethargy. In frosty weather they usually lie low, sometimes for days at a time, but come back on the feed as the water grows warmer. One scientifically-minded fisherman has written a book to show that they are at their most voracious when the temperature of the water is rising through about 42° to 44° Fahrenheit. Then (he says) they will take anything—a lump of cheese, or some poor little duckling, a water rat, or a spinner made from the end of an old toothbrush or a lady's ornamental hat-pin. In autumn the biggest pike, the females, are sluggish, for at this time of year they are preparing to spawn. (A pike's hatch of eggs may well weigh several pounds, and naturally this extra weight tells on their condition.) In January and February, however, they will fight much harder and may well break a fisherman's tackle by their sheer weight and strength. It is worth while to catch a few, just to get them out of the water, for they are like water-tigers to the smaller fish, hunting and devouring with their great (and terribly sharp) teeth, and thus doing harm to a well-stocked river.

Of all the water birds to be seen on a lake, among the most arresting and beautiful must surely be the great crested grebe. His appearance is so unusual that even people who are not particularly interested in birds will often point out over the water and ask what he is. He has a wide, brown ruff of feathers framing his white face, and a double, rosette-shaped crest on the crown of his head. Long-necked and about as big as a duck, he paddles slowly and methodically up a lake, stabbing and dipping for food, in his odd appearance rather like some strange and beautiful toy. One very seldom sees many grebes together: they tend to be solitary, and also wary and timid. In a way, it is inappropriate to mention them as part of the lake scene in winter, for they are migrants, arriving in this country in March and leaving about October or early November, though during a mild winter they may remain later.

To watch duck arriving and feeding on an inland sheet of water is always exciting—widgeon, pochard and gadwall, teal, shoveler, pintail and many more. They are well worth learning to recognize. There is not space here for more than a hint at their variety and beauty—but binoculars, gumboots, warm clothes, a good bird-book and a reasonable amount of patience will open the marvellous world—our own world, though unknown to many people—in which these gallant, splendid creatures carry on their lives and make their long migratory flights over the curved world. If it freezes hard, then however fond of skating you may be, break a part of the ice for them; and throw in some bread, too. It's their lake more than ours—they need it more—and a frosty winter night requires a full crop before darkness falls.

Key to Illustration on pages 100-101

ANIMALS

1 Kingfisher 2 Whooper swan 3 Heron 4 Moorhen 5 Mallard (male) 6 Mallard (female) 7 Pochard

PLANTS AND TREES

8 Oak 9 Willow (pollarded) 10 Alders 11 Reeds 12 Reedmace (bulrush) 13 Hawthorn

Temperature Control

Temperature is of immense importance to animals, since it controls the speed of chemical reactions in the body. These chemical reactions provide energy, and so the whole energy of the animal depends on temperature. If you watch a frog swimming in a pond, you will see that the actions of its legs are controlled by muscles which depend on chemical reactions. If the water is icy, these chemical reactions are slower and the frog swims less fast. In warmer water the reactions are faster and the frog swims faster.

Frogs are cold-blooded animals, which means that they cannot control their own temperatures as we can, but keep at the same temperature as the surrounding air or water. Cold-blooded animals are at a disadvantage in very hot and very cold climates. In hot conditions the chemical reactions go too fast and exhaust the animal, and in cold conditions they are so slow that the animal can hardly function at all.

Mammals and birds are warm-blooded and so can escape these problems by having systems for keeping their body temperature at more or less the same level despite the temperature outside. To be able to do this they have to be able to store heat when cold and get rid of it when hot. Unfortunately these two requirements can work against each other. For example, mammals have fur and birds have feathers. These keep them warm in cold climates, and even in hot climates they help to stop too much heat entering the body, since fur and feathers are good 'insulators'. But with bodies covered with such good insulating materials, once the heat has entered the bodies mammals and birds find it difficult to push it out again. To overcome this, they push out water—in the form of sweat— instead. This evaporates, and cools the body.

The ears of rabbits and hares are very well supplied with blood vessels, and these, because they lie close beneath the skin, enable the animals to disperse extra body heat to the surrounding air in hot weather. The Arizona jack-rabbit, because it lives in a hot desert region, has very long ears; compare them with those of the European rabbit (above) who lives in a temperate climate.

Sparrows, like other birds, fluff up their feathers in cold weather. This creates a layer of air between the skin and the surrounding atmosphere. Air is an excellent insulator and so preserves the body warmth of the birds.

The blue whale has up to 18 in. of blubber beneath its skin. This allows the internal temperature to stay constant, even in the coldest waters. Its flukes and fins, on the other hand, have no blubber and, where their temperature is lower than the internal temperature, their complex interlacing veins and arteries allow enough heat to be circulated through them to supply the necessary warmth to their muscles.

The most important system of control on mammals is through the bloodstream. The tiny blood vessels in the skin contract in cold weather. This means that less blood gets to the skin so the skin gets colder. But the rest of the body benefits, for by less blood flowing to the skin, less blood gets cold and so less cold blood flows back into the body. Sometimes animals have *arteries* (which carry blood away from the heart) and *veins* (which carry blood to the heart) intertwined, so that heat can flow between them. An extremity will remain cool in hot weather, but still receive oxygen if heat passes from artery to vein.

Whales, which of course are warm-blooded mammals, though they look a bit like fish, have a blood system which pumps blood to the tail and flippers and consists of a large artery surrounded by a spiral of small veins. When cold blood returns from the tail or flippers in the veins it is heated by the arteries. The heat is kept within the animal rather than being dispersed into the sea.

Most mammals do not have such extremes to contend with. They can fluff out their hairs (or in the case of birds their feathers), which provide an insulating layer of air, or they can shiver. Their skin blood vessels contract and these actions are usually enough to keep warm-blooded animals warm.

Mammals can build up layers of fat beneath the skin to shield them against very cold temperatures. Cold-blooded animals are more interesting. Fish can get used to higher temperatures in one day and lower temperatures in three weeks. Animals living in water are better at doing this very quick adjustment than ones that live on land. But snails and some insects, such as cockroaches, can perform this very quick change to different temperatures.

INDEX

Boldface page numbers refer to the Keys for the large landscape illustrations. *Italic* page numbers refer to other illustrations and to captions. Roman numbers refer to text.

water rail, *Rallus aquaticus*, 25
water spider, *Argyroneta aquatica*, 56
water violet, *Hottonia palustris*, **27, 51**
waterwort, *Elatine hexandra*, **51**
waved umber moth, *Menophra abruptaria*, 94
western juniper, *Juniperus occidentalis*, 80
whale (Cetacea), 103
wheat, *Triticum*, 15, 18, **19**, 22, *23*
white bark pine, *Pinus albicaulis*, 80
white bryony, *Bryonia dioica*, 65
white campion, *Silene alba*, **67**
White, Gilbert, 66
whites (Pieridae), *16*
whooper swan, *Cygnus cygnus*, 25, **99**
wild arum, *Arum maculatum*, 18, 38
wild celery, *Apium graveolens*, 22
wild rye, *Elymus glaucus*, 80
wild service tree, *Sorbus torminalis*, 65
willow-herb, *Epilobium*, 46, 63
willow, *Salix fragilis*, **27, 51, 75, 99**
willow warbler, *Phylloscopus trochilus*,
66, 74
winter aconite, *Eranthis hyemalis*, 38,
83, 91
winter moth, *Operophtera brumata*, 40
witches' butter, *Exidia glandulosa*, 59
woad, *Isatis tinctoria*, 67
wood anemone, *Anemone nemorosa*,
10, **11**, *15*
wood avens, *Geum urbanum*, 62, 63
wood false brome grass, *Brachypodium
salvaticum*, **83**
wood melick, *Melica uniflora*, **83**
wood mouse, *Apodemus sylvaticus*, 46
wood pigeon, *Columba palumbus*, 42, **43**
wood sedge, *Carex sylvatica*, **59**
wood sorrel, *Oxalis acetosella*, **11, 59**, 62
wood white, *Leptidea sinapis*, **11, 35**
wood meadow-grass, *Poa nemoralis*, 14.
14, 18, 83
woody nightshade, *Solanum dulcamara*, 65
worker bee, *48*
wren, *Troglodytes troglodytes*, 24
wych elm, *Ulmus glabra*, **11, 35, 59, 83**

yarrow, *Achillea millefolium*, 42
yellow chamomile, *Anthemis tinctoria*, **43**
yellow hammer, *Emberiza citrinella*, *19*
yellow-tail, *Euproctis similis*, *17*
yellow water-lily, *Nuphar lutea*, **51**
yew, *Taxus baccata*, 39

Units of length

1 in	—	2·540 cm
1 ft	—	30·48 cm
1 yd	—	0·9144 m
1 mile	—	1·609 km
1 cm	—	0·3937 in
1 m	—	3·281 ft
1 m	—	1·094 yd
1 km	—	0·6214 mile

Temperatures

Centigrade		Fahrenheit
°C 1	—	33°F
5	—	41
10	—	50
15	—	59
20	—	68
25	—	77
30	—	86
35	—	95
40	—	104
45	—	113
50	—	122